The Barefoot Eulogist

Speaking a Good Word While Standing on Holy Ground

Bruce C. Salmon

© 2022

Published in the United States by Nurturing Faith, Macon, Ga.

Nurturing Faith is a book imprint of Good Faith Media (goodfaithmedia.org).

Library of Congress Cataloging-in-Publication Data is available.

ISBN 978-1-63528-204-7

All rights reserved. Printed in the United States of America.

Unless otherwise indicated, all scripture citations
come from the New Revised Standard Version (NRSV).

Cover and interior design by Amy C. Cook.

Cover image from Vecteezy.com

"In an age where most people turn away from the burning bush of the sacred ignited by death, Bruce Salmon confidently, competently, and compassionately moves toward the holy ground of grief and loss where God is revealed amidst the cries of the people. Unafraid of his own tears and the unspeakable pain of others, in this book he offers not only a technical 'how-to' manual for the professional pastoral practice of conducting a funeral in myriad circumstances, but also with engaging prose he tacitly transmits the personal presence necessary to bring a healing stability at the point of life's greatest disruption. In so doing, he demonstrates how the practice of pastoral care can bring together theological expertise and psychological awareness to provide a vital spiritual and mental health safety net in our communities, without which our culture will fall apart. For those with their feet on the ground in the practice of congregational and community care, this book is a must read."—Thomas E. Rodgerson, Consultant, Centrepointe Counseling Inc.; Author, *Overhearing a Christian Apology to the Nones*

"The first time I put together a funeral service, I felt clueless. The weight of trying to honor a life well lived and minister to a grieving community can seem insurmountable to a new pastor. The greatest gift I received was samples and guidance from a ministry mentor who had already been around the block. In *The Barefoot Eulogist*, Bruce Salmon has become that mentor for pastors like me in my first days, sitting at a blank screen praying God will provide a 'good word.' Salmon offers wisdom from more than three decades in ministry, during which he was faced with the task of preaching eulogies for young children, dear friends, and even family members. His examples and reflections are an unparalleled resource for pastors of all stripes. I know the pages of my copy will become well-loved through the years to come!"—Emily Holladay, Pastor, Village Baptist Church, Bowie, Md.

"*The Barefoot Eulogist* is a great read and a great resource for those tasked with offering a funeral elegy. Eulogizing is one of the most difficult tasks in ministry, and there is precious little literature to help. Bruce Salmon has given all of us a gift with a sampling of eulogies he has delivered through the years, accompanied by reflections that are like mini-tutorials. They each reflect careful preparation and compassionate presentation. Each eulogy is different, yet each is a 'good word' that not only offers insight into those eulogized but also into the heart of a skilled pastor. What impressed me with these eulogies is a careful attention to details in one's life that are then spoken with care. I especially benefited from Bruce's numerous descriptions of a eulogy and then his demonstration of how it's done with integrity. This book belongs in the library of all who consider a eulogy for someone, or for themselves."—Daniel Vestal, Distinguished Professor of Baptist Leadership, Director of the Eula Mae and John Baugh Center for Baptist Leadership, Mercer University

Contents

Introduction vii

Chapter 1: Giving Voice to Our Grief 1
Eulogy for Jeff Kurtz
Reflections

Chapter 2: Telling the Story 11
Eulogy for Patricia (Patsy) West
Reflections

Chapter 3: Lifting Up Our Christian Hope 19
Eulogy for Jo Reiter
Reflections

Chapter 4: Gone Too Soon 27
Remembering Bodhi
Reflections

Chapter 5: Sudden Loss 35
Eulogy for Rick and Amelia Dashiell
Reflections

Chapter 6: The Prime of Life 49
Eulogy for Peter Franklyn
Reflections

Chapter 7: Complicated Grief 55
Eulogy for Ron Knode
Reflections

Chapter 8: Personal Grief 63
Eulogy for Skip Ford
Reflections

Chapter 9: Well Done... 77
Eulogy for Zenobia Mae Fenrick
Reflections

Chapter 10: The Rest of the Story 83
Eulogy for Jim Langley
Reflections

Chapter 11: Mother of a Friend... 95
Eulogy for Agnes Cheri
Reflections

Chapter 12: Benediction 103
Remembering Maury Sweetin
Reflections

Chapter 13: At the Cemetery 109
Committal Service for Ann Rakes
Reflections

Chapter 14: Continuing Ministry... 117
Eulogy for Kathleen (Kat) Garvin
Reflections

About the Author... 127

Introduction

Eulogy is derived from the Greek *eu* and *logos*, meaning "good word." A eulogy is a good word about a person who has died, usually spoken during a funeral or memorial service, or sometimes at a graveside committal service. During my 33 years as pastor of Village Baptist Church in Bowie, Maryland, I delivered many eulogies for church members, former church members, family of church members, and other persons in the community. Over the years I also have given eulogies for my own family members: my grandmother, my sister-in-law, my father, my sister, and my brother-in-law. Serving as a eulogist is one of my most important and meaningful ministries.

The purpose of a eulogy is at least threefold: to give voice to our grief, to remember the person who has died, and to lift up our Christian hope. My goal in writing and delivering the eulogy is to tell the story of the person with honesty and compassion, and to comfort the family and friends with the assurance of God's presence and our hope of life eternal.

A eulogy can include reflections on passages of scripture, but the focus is on the individual who is being remembered and on our Christian hope in the face of loss. Unlike sermons where I often use illustrations from my own life, eulogies tell the stories of someone else, and I seek to minimize my own footprints, except in relationship to the person being remembered.

Eulogies are more reflective and less didactic than sermons. They invite us to reflect upon the lives of persons no longer with us, but whose influence is still being felt. Eulogies seek the presence of God in the aftermath of loss. They speak a good word both about the persons remembered and about the God who holds them—and us.

I approach every eulogy with the assumption that the person who died is now within God's care. That assumption does not diminish the importance of faith or righteous living. But it acknowledges that God is merciful, and it is not ours to judge. I approach every eulogy with the belief that this world and this life are not all there is. Yet, this world and this life matter. The person who died matters. Our relationship with that person matters. God understands our grief, and God will help us to deal with our loss.

The eulogist speaks for the person who is no longer with us, and for the family and friends of that person, and yes, the eulogist speaks for God. It is an awesome responsibility to speak for others, and yet it can be done. Even if I know the person who had died, I seek to learn as much about that person as I can.

Sometimes I meet with family members and ask them to talk about their loved one. I sit among them with pen and paper in hand and take notes. Other times I ask family members to write a timeline of the person's life, with as many details as they want to give. Sometimes I solicit written testimonies from those who knew the person, or I incorporate remembrances that are submitted on the obituary page of the funeral home's web site. The more I can find out about the person, the more complete my story of that person's life will be.

In speaking for God, I rely heavily on passages of scripture that relate to our mortality and God's faithfulness, and the consequences of the resurrection of Jesus Christ from the dead. Often, I will read some of those passages during the funeral or memorial service as a prelude to the eulogy. Sometimes I will quote passages during the eulogy to offer reassurance and affirmation of life after death. Those scriptures inform my own understanding of eternal life. A eulogy is more than a biography of what has been; it is an expression of faith in what is to come.

The purpose of this book is to provide examples of eulogies I have given, in the hope that these examples might help other eulogists in the art and craft of writing tributes to those who have died, provide consolation for those who are grieving, and lift up the Christian promise of eternal life.

Surviving family members have given me permission to share these eulogies of their loved ones, both as a way to remember them and to help others. At the conclusion of each chapter, I offer some reflections on the eulogy given, as a way of prompting the reader to reflect on how it was crafted and how the basic principles of writing a eulogy can be adapted to each particular circumstance.

When writing a eulogy, I insert space between each sentence/thought to encourage myself to slow down during delivery and to allow time for the listeners to hear and reflect. Unlike sermons where I will sometimes depart from the manuscript during delivery, I try to present eulogies as close to the manuscript as possible. That is because I carefully write them to include pertinent details of the person's life, and I do not want to skip over any of those details for the sake of spontaneity.

I titled this book *The Barefoot Eulogist* because speaking a good word about any person created in the image of God is holy work. Every time I deliver a eulogy, I take off my shoes (figuratively), because I am standing on holy ground (Exod. 3:5, Josh. 5:15, Acts 7:33).

Chapter 1
Giving Voice to Our Grief

Grief is a part of life. If you live long enough, you will lose someone you love. Mourning is a necessary step to resuming life after loss. Every culture has developed rituals of mourning to help the bereaved begin to work through their grief and to get on with their lives. Funerals and memorial services are important rituals of mourning that help facilitate the grieving process.

The COVID pandemic, beginning in 2020, disrupted many aspects of our lives, including our rituals of mourning. During the early days of the pandemic, I gave eulogies for seven people who had died. Three of those eulogies were delivered during virtual memorial services on computer screens. Four were given during in-person funerals at cemeteries or at funeral homes, with attendees wearing face masks and endeavoring to stay socially distanced. In the cases of three other friends who died during the pandemic, there was no funeral or memorial service. I was in touch with surviving family members, and we discussed the options of conducting a virtual or in-person service, and they decided to delay a time of remembrance to a later date.

Frankly, neither the virtual memorial service nor the touchless in-person funeral was a fully satisfying experience. It was good to see people's faces on the computer screen and to talk with them, and it was not difficult to stay socially distanced since we were already physically distanced, but it was not the same as being with them. Similarly, it was good to be with people in person, but since we could not see each other unmasked, or get close to each other, or touch each other, funeral services during the pandemic were stilted, awkward, and not fully satisfying.

During times of grief, we want to see and touch each other, to embrace, to shake hands, to hold hands, to physically console. Making eye contact while wearing face masks is not the same as seeing the full facial expression. While the face masks were a necessary barrier to help prevent the spread of the virus, they also inhibited interaction and meaningful community.

Those experiences early in the pandemic reminded me of the importance of in-person funerals and memorial services. In the aftermath of loss, we need to be together to share our grief and to begin the process of healing. The eulogy is an important part of that process, for it provides an opportunity to reflect upon the life of the person we are remembering. But other parts of the funeral or memorial service are important, too.

Most services include prayer, scripture readings, and music. Sometimes an obituary is read, or people are invited to share remembrances. Often there are photos either displayed or projected. There may be a printed program with a photo on the cover, an order of service, and perhaps a listing of surviving family members. Sometimes poetry is included on the program or read during the service or at the graveside committal. The goal is to make the service relevant to the person being remembered and meaningful for those who are participating.

The amount and nature of religious content in the service also are related to the person being remembered and those who are participating. Funerals and memorial services are not "one size fits all." Nevertheless, even for those without a church relationship, my assumption has been that asking clergy to officiate is a sign that some religious content is expected and would be appreciated. Thus, every funeral and memorial service I officiate includes prayer, scripture reading, and affirmation of our Christian hope.

The Bible contains many passages that could be used in funeral and memorial services. Below are some scriptures that I or family members or friends have read:

- Deuteronomy 33:27
- Nehemiah 8:10
- Job 19:25-27
- Psalm 23
- Psalm 46:1-5, 7, 10-11
- Psalm 86:5-7
- Psalm 90:1-12
- Psalm 121
- Isaiah 25:6-9
- Isaiah 40:28-31
- John 3:16
- John 11:25-26
- John 14:1-6, 27

Giving Voice to Our Grief

- Romans 8:14-23, 31-39
- Romans 14:8
- 1 Corinthians 15:51-57
- 2 Corinthians 4:16-18
- 2 Corinthians 5:1, 4-5
- Philippians 4:11-13
- 1 Thessalonians 4:13-18
- 2 Timothy 4:7-8
- 1 Peter 1:3-9
- 1 Peter 5:1-11
- Jude 24-25
- Revelation 22:12-14

The singing of hymns is common in many funerals and memorial services, especially those that are conducted in a church. Below is a list of some hymns that have been used. Again, the list is not exhaustive.

- "Abide with Me"
- "Amazing Grace! How Sweet the Sound"
- "Be Thou My Vision"
- "Because He Lives"
- "Blessed Assurance, Jesus Is Mine"
- "Blest Be the Tie"
- "Eternal Father, Strong to Save"
- "Give Me Jesus"
- "God Be with You"
- "Great Is Thy Faithfulness"
- "He Is My Peace"
- "How Great Thou Art"
- "I Know That My Redeemer Lives!"
- "In Christ Alone"
- "In the Garden"
- "It Is Well with My Soul"
- "Jesus, Keep Me Near the Cross"
- "Leaning on the Everlasting Arms"

- "Morning Has Broken"
- "My Faith Looks Up to Thee"
- "Near to the Heart of God"
- "Pass Me Not, O Gentle Savior"
- "Precious Lord, Take My Hand"
- "Rock of Ages, Cleft for Me"
- "Softly and Tenderly"
- "The Solid Rock"
- "To God Be the Glory"
- "What a Friend We Have in Jesus"
- "When We All Get to Heaven"
- "You Are My All in All"

A printed program often contains the order of service and a listing of family members. It may include a picture on the front cover and a poem or scripture passage on the back cover. Sometimes the printed program includes the obituary from the funeral home web site, either on the inside or back, or as an insert.

Often in funeral or memorial services, vocal or instrumental music is included. Some of the more popular solos include "His Eye Is on the Sparrow," "The Lord's Prayer," "On Eagle's Wings," "Amazing Grace," "When I Get Where I'm Going," "In My Father's House Are Many Mansions," and "The Old Rugged Cross."

Sometimes before the service there will be a time of visitation when friends come to share condolences with the family and view the body in the casket. Often after the service the church hosts a repast or a reception in the fellowship hall. Both the visitation before the service and the repast/reception after the service provide opportunities for support on a more personal level. All these elements facilitate the ritual of mourning: photos, scripture readings, prayers, poetry, reading the obituary, testimonies, remembrances, solos, congregational singing, instrumental tributes, and the eulogy.

All this changed in 2020–2021. In-person funerals came to a halt, and we learned a new ritual of virtual memorial services. I gave my first virtual eulogy in May of 2020. It was for a friend from our former church who died of COVID-19, Jeff Kurtz. His wife, Cecelia, was a member of our church before she ever met Jeff. But after they connected, Cecelia began to bring Jeff to church with her, and we became friends. They asked me to officiate their wedding. Rather than getting married in our church building, though,

Cecelia and Jeff planned a destination wedding on Tybee Island in Georgia over the 4th of July weekend. My wife Linda and I flew to Charleston, South Carolina, rented a car, and drove down to Tybee, off the coast of Savannah. The wedding was held outside in front of the lighthouse, with a reception inside. There we met most of Jeff's and Cecelia's families. It was a storybook affair.

After I retired in 2018, we maintained contact with Cecelia and Jeff. We joined them for dinner on a couple of occasions, and Jeff was trying to find a time when he and I could play golf at Congressional Country Club, where he was a member. We had exchanged emails in November of 2019 about renovations to one of the golf courses at Congressional, and we discussed possibly playing the other course when the weather improved. Then the pandemic hit. Life as we knew it shut down.

Cecelia contacted me later in the spring of 2020 with tragic news. Jeff had died from COVID-19. Cecelia, a nurse, had unknowingly brought the virus home from the hospital. She and Jeff had gotten sick on the same day. Cecelia recovered after two weeks, but Jeff ended up in the hospital, where he died a month later. Jeff was still fully employed, a tennis player, a bicyclist, a frequent traveler. But such is the nature of the virus. Some infected people are asymptomatic, some recover from the illness, and others die. Due to COVID-19, 2020 was the deadliest year in U.S. history. Jeff was the first person I knew who died from the virus. Unfortunately, I would go on to know others. What follows is the eulogy I gave during the virtual memorial service for Jeff Kurtz.

Eulogy for Jeff Kurtz
May 24, 2020

I want to thank Cecelia for giving me the opportunity to offer this eulogy for Jeff. Eulogy comes from the Greek, meaning "good word," and I have a good word to speak about Jeff Kurtz. Jeff was a friend of mine, and I will talk more about that later, but first let me give an overview of Jeff's life, based on the timeline that Cecelia provided.

Jeffrey Robert Kurtz was born on August 28, 1948, in Oakland, California. His parents were William Edward Kurtz and Dorothy Ruth Kurtz. His father was a pilot in the United States Navy. Jeff and his older brother Mike moved all over the U.S. during their father's Navy career. Jeff recalled living in California in a house that overlooked a cliff where watermelons grew. Eventually, when Jeff was around eight years of age, the family settled in Somerset, Maryland, a town bordered by Bethesda on one side and Washington, D.C. on the other.

Jeff attended Somerset Elementary and Westland Junior High School. He told stories about studying at the Little Falls Branch Library and playing football with his friends on open fields that are now roads and townhomes in the area. After junior high, Jeff attended boarding school at St. James Episcopal in Hagerstown, Maryland. After graduation, he attended DePauw University, where he studied history and joined the Lambda Chi Alpha fraternity. Jeff graduated in 1971 with the Bachelor of Arts degree.

For a time, Jeff wasn't sure what he was going to do. He loved history, but it's hard to make a career from that. In the early 1970s, Jeff began working for the District Department of Labor under the federal auspices of the U.S. Department of Labor. He was an analyst for youth obtaining employment in the District during the summer months. It was during this time that Jeff enrolled at American University, where he earned his Master of Public Administration degree.

Between his part-time employment with the federal government, working as a waiter to make ends meet, and graduate school, Jeff found time to travel. He made a trip to Europe, mostly to visit an au pair he had met in D.C. Imagine that! By his 30s, Jeff's career in the federal government was well on its way. He had jobs with the Drug Enforcement Agency and with the State Department. He traveled to North Africa, Southeast Asia, and throughout the U.S. He worked for the Farmers Home Administration and with a federal agency that worked with contractors who hired people with physical disabilities. Finally, Jeff found his way to the U.S. Department of Agriculture where he would work for the rest of his career.

Jeff experienced more than his share of ups and downs in his life. In the late 1980s, Jeff lost his wife and unborn son. But in the early 90s he found love again, which resulted in the birth of his two daughters, Jackie and Niki. Unfortunately, that marriage ended in divorce. Yet, Jeff remained very involved in raising his children. He was a great provider and a great father. He raised his daughters to be disciplined and independent. He loved them without end. They were the best thing that ever happened to Jeff; that is, until Cecelia came along.

Jeff met Cecelia back in 2010. On September 17, he sent her an email with the subject line, "My lucky day." It was a lucky day for both of them. Jeff asked Cecelia to go out on a date. That led to a two-hour phone conversation that day, then another two-hour phone conversation the next day. Then it was a five-hour date two days later. They couldn't get enough of each other. This went on for over a year until early in 2012 when Cecelia moved in with him. Yep, they were "living in sin," until they got married on July 3, 2014.

Sometime after they started dating, I got to know Jeff. Cecelia brought him with her to church, and she introduced him to me one Sunday morning. This was a big sacrifice for Jeff because he usually played tennis at Congressional Country Club on Sunday mornings. But over time, Jeff started coming to church more and more often, and I got to know him better and better. I really liked him. He was a good guy. It wasn't until Cecelia told me they wanted to get married that I began to have any doubts about their relationship. You see, Jeff was older than Cecelia, and I wondered if they had thought things through. They asked me to marry them, and during several months of premarital counseling, I raised the issue of their age difference. But as we met, I came to understand more about their connection with one another. I came to see the character of the man that Jeff was, his kindness and his compassion and his heart for others. At first, when Cecelia got involved with a man older than she, I was concerned that she might be getting into more than she bargained for. But as I saw how the two of them related to each other, I came to better understand the love that drew them together.

Their wedding took place at the Tybee Island Lighthouse and Cottage on Tybee Island, Georgia on July 3, 2014. It was my honor to officiate the ceremony and to meet most of Jeff's family and Cecelia's family. My wife Linda was there too. It was a great occasion, despite Cecelia's grandmother getting stuck in an elevator on the way up to the dinner after the ceremony. It didn't really bother her—she just laughed it off. At the beginning of the wedding ceremony, we heard a song by John Legend, a love song. In the song John Legend sang,

> 'Cause all of me
> Loves all of you
> Loves your curves and all your edges
> All your perfect imperfections
> Give your all to me
> I'll give my all to you
> You're my end and my beginnin'
> Even when I lose, I'm winnin'
>
> 'Cause I give you all of me
> And you give me all of you.

That song reflected the theme of their life together. They gave their all to each other. And they had fun doing it. They traveled to Europe several times. They drove down the California coast. They sailed the Caribbean. They walked the streets of Charleston and Savannah. They took a train trip through the Canadian Rockies. They dug their toes in the sand in Sarasota. They went to plays, baseball games, music concerts at Strathmore—not to mention museums where they would spend hours at exhibits. The point is, they had so much in common. They both loved learning and learning from other people.

The neighbors won't forget seeing Jeff riding his bike through Carderock with Cecelia or riding alone just enjoying the sunshine. I mentioned about Jeff playing tennis. He loved it. He would play two to three times a week. He looked forward to the World Team Tennis event every summer. But even though he was a member of Congressional Country Club, Jeff did not like to play golf. Yet, he told me he was willing to play one round with me. For several years we discussed making that happen. Jeff even went so far as to contact the pro shop at Congressional about setting up a tee time for us. That's when he learned that if he were to bring me as a guest to play golf at Congressional, we would have to hire caddies in order for me to play. Now, I love playing with a caddy. I've done it several times in Ireland, and once in South Africa. But playing with a caddy in America is EXPENSIVE. I can only imagine what it would cost at Congressional. So, I told Jeff to wait and maybe we could find a time to play at Congressional without a caddy. Maybe we could play on the other course or play during the off-season.

Last November Jeff sent me an email about the reconstruction of the Blue course at Congressional, a $25 million project. He told me the project could take as long as one and a half years, which meant that golfers are being forced to wait for tee times and play the other (Gold) course. Well, that didn't bother Jeff. He reminded me, "I'm a tennis player." I replied that I had been able to play the Blue course some years ago, and that I've been wanting to play the Gold course. I told him I had an extra set of clubs that he could use. Then I told him about our visiting my mother in Texas last year. Jeff wrote me back, and he said that my visiting my mother in Texas had inspired him to visit his stepmother in Sarasota, Florida. He said they had made airline reservations and were going to visit her the next month. He also told me about the trip they took out to Vancouver last July, and how they boarded the "Rocky Mountaineer" for a train trip through the Canadian Rockies.

Jeff and I never got to play our round of golf together at Congressional. It's like our friendship was interrupted, ended far too soon. That's the way all of us feel. Our relationship with Jeff ended far too soon. We loved him, and we miss him. But we are so grateful to have known him. Jeff Kurtz was a special person, and we will never forget him. Now, we've got to find a way to carry on without him. God will help us to carry on, if we place our trust in him. One thing, though, we don't have to worry about is Jeff. We know that he is safe and secure with God in heaven. Now, I don't know if there are any tennis courts in heaven, but if there are, Jeff has probably already played a set, or even two.

Reflections

Because I wrote the eulogy for Jeff Kurtz early in the pandemic, I was unable to sit down with family members before the memorial service to talk about Jeff. I did talk with his wife Cecelia several times on the phone, and we exchanged several emails. I asked Cecelia to provide a timeline of Jeff's life, and that was the basis for the first part of the eulogy. Then I moved from telling the story of Jeff's life to telling the story of the kind of person Jeff was. I wove into that narrative my own relationship with Jeff, and especially my remembrances of their destination wedding that Jeff and Cecelia had invited me to officiate. I was able to use some recent email exchanges that I had with Jeff to bring our relationship into the present and to reflect upon the person I had come to know him to be.

Under normal circumstances, I might have sought input from Jeff's two daughters to provide a more complete portrait of their father. But since we could not meet in person, and since time was limited, and since this was the first virtual memorial service for all of us, I used Cecelia's timeline as the basis for the chronology of Jeff's life.

Cecelia and Jeff's daughters did put together a "printed" program with many pictures and an obituary and the order of service that was sent as an email attachment to those who had been invited to the Zoom memorial service. The program included photos of Jeff and Cecelia at their wedding, photos of Jeff with his daughters, a photo of Jeff with his tennis buddies, a photo of Jeff on his bicycle, and photos of Jeff and Cecelia on some of their travels. So, the printed program helped tell the story too.

Chapter 2
Telling the Story

I read obituaries in the newspaper. An obituary is different from a newspaper death notice. The death notice is a paid entry written by the family. It announces to the community that someone has died, and it presents an overview of that person's life. An obituary in the newspaper is not purchased by the family. It is written by a paid member of the newspaper staff. Both the death notice and the obituary tell the story of the person's life, but the death notice tells the story from the perspective of the family, while the obituary tells the story from the perspective of an unrelated observer.

Sometimes the newspaper obituary is longer than the death notice, and it tells the story from a particular point of view. While the death notice seeks to relate the totality of a person's life, the obituary focuses on a particular achievement or reason for notoriety. Almost anyone can have a death notice published in the newspaper, but obituaries are written for persons of renown or celebrity or curiosity. Only a small percentage of those who have died have an obituary written about them in the newspaper. Most death notices are sympathetic toward the person being remembered, while most newspaper obituaries aim to be accurate and factual.

The eulogy is neither a death notice nor an obituary, but it too seeks to tell the story of the person who is being remembered. Like the death notice, the eulogy seeks to be sympathetic, and like the newspaper obituary, the eulogy seeks to be accurate and factual. My aim in writing the eulogy is to tell the story with compassion and honesty.

Learning the story of the person who has died is important preparation for telling the story. In some cases, I knew the person well. In other cases, I did not know the person at all. But in all cases I seek to gain as much information as possible to tell the story of that person's life. To learn more about the deceased, sometimes I sit down with the family and ask them to tell me about their loved one. I listen carefully and take notes. Sometimes I ask a key family member to write a timeline of their loved one's life, with such information as when and where the person was born, the family of origin, childhood experiences, education, work, interests, relationships, etc. Sometimes a family member will write a chronology, including personal remembrances and reflections. Sometimes family members and friends will email their remembrances to me.

During the early days of the pandemic, I gave the eulogy for a virtual memorial service for the sister of one of our best friends who had died of COVID-19. I knew the sister: we had been together for a couple of golf trips, and I had been with her on a few other occasions. But my relationship with her was more occasional than consistent. So, I needed more information. I asked her daughter to write a timeline of her mother's life and to solicit remembrances from other family members. The daughter did so, gathering memories including a tribute from her mother's former pastor. I also went to the funeral home obituary web page and garnered remembrances that various family members and friends had written there. Then I wove together the remembrances and tributes from many of those family members and friends into the eulogy, and added a few personal ones. By including material from many others, I was able to present a more complete picture. The daughter of the deceased, Chris Gedney, gave me permission to share the eulogy I wrote for her mother.

Eulogy for Patricia (Patsy) West
January 30, 2021

I want to thank Chris for giving me the opportunity to offer this eulogy for her mother. Patsy was a friend of mine, and I will talk more about that later, but first let me give an overview of her life, based on the timeline that Chris provided, and on an email that Patsy sent me back in 2008.

Patricia Anne was born on December 20, 1933, in Queens, NY. She was the second child of Leslie and Elsie Short. Her big brother was Donald Short, and her little sister was Leslie Short [Parreco]. Patsy grew up in Baldwin, New York, on Long Island. She went to Baldwin High School, but she left before graduating to pursue a job in New York City at the age of only 17. During her high school days Patsy was invited to a party by a boy she was not really interested in dating. But her mother told her, "Just go to the party; you never know who you will meet." Well, it turned out the boy throwing the party was named Fred West. Patsy went to the party, and she and Fred began dating, and eventually they became engaged. But after a fight on the phone, they broke up, and they went on to marry other spouses.

Patsy met Charlie Gedney, who was working as a tech writer for her father, at a beach party on Long Island. After a short six-week romance, they were married in 1955 and left for Santa Monica, California right after the

Telling the Story

ceremony. They moved to California for Charlie's work, but after only a year on the West Coast, Patsy became pregnant and wanted to go "home" to Long Island to be near her family. Patsy and Charlie went on to have three children: Tim, Chris, and Anne.

During the early years of their marriage, they lived on Long Island. They enjoyed time with family and friends on Jones Beach, traveling to Fire Island, taking trips to Lake George, and other outings. Because Patsy was very close to her mom, she wanted to raise the children near their grandparents, and they did so, both on Long Island, and in Maryland, when her parents and younger sister, Leslie, moved there. They bought a townhouse in Gaithersburg, and later they bought a large, lovely home in Rockville.

Patsy worked for over 15 years in the Montgomery County school system as a processing center support person. She loved her work friends. Many were ladies living in the Aspen Hill neighborhood, which made it easy for social activities outside of work. Patsy was always home when the kids left for school, and she was always there when they got home from school. Being a mother and a homemaker was priority number one. Patsy was a huge supporter of her kids' activities while they were growing up. She attended Tim's diving events in high school, and Chris's basketball and softball games. Patsy and Charlie would drive to Connecticut to watch Chris play basketball for UConn. She wore "UConn Mom" tee shirts and proudly talked about the games to anyone who was willing to listen.

Her daughter Anne shared these thoughts about her mother:

> My parents always made sure we had a wonderful Christmas when I was growing up. I remember beautiful Christmas trees with lots of presents under the tree. One year I even got an Easy Bake Oven, and I was so excited. I remember family vacations to Vermont in the summers and one that was especially memorable was when my godparents, Betty Jane and Bob, and their kids went with us. My mom always took me shopping for new clothes prior to the first day of school. It was a tradition! My mom and I gardened together when she was living in Newport News. We were successful at growing broccoli, carrots, and lettuce in our garden and were proud of our harvest. I am thankful she is pain free and at peace now.

In her early 40s, Patsy took up running. She had been a smoker for decades, but one day she just decided to quit. She ran numerous 10k races, and she even completed the 13.1-mile Bay to Breakers run in San Francisco. She enjoyed just being out in nature, and the "runner's high" of feeling her legs propel her with strength and determination. She also loved flowers, and she had one of the best gardens in her neighborhoods for most of her adult life. Patsy was an artist, mastering pencil sketching later in life, and she was an avid photographer, entering her pictures in local craft shows. Patsy also played golf for many years.

In 1996 and in 1999 Patsy and her second husband, Fred, joined us on our annual winter golf trip, along with Leslie and Pete. In 1996 Patsy and Fred went with us to South Carolina. We started out in Charleston, then we went to the Kiawah Island Golf Resort. In 1999 Patsy and Fred joined us at the Sedona Golf Resort in Arizona. It was fun having them with us. Patsy also loved dogs, and she would often dog-sit for neighbors' dogs, while having several dogs of her own for years.

Patsy's biggest love was her love of children. She simply adored kids—her kids, her grandkids, her great-grandkids. She would walk up to strangers to compliment the baby or child. Maybe it was her own childlike wonder that drew her to children. They would respond in kind with a cute smile or a chuckle or just hold her gaze for a few moments. Children brought her immense joy.

Patsy also found joy by the ocean. She and Charlie owned a beach house on Rehoboth Bay in Delaware during the late 70s and 80s. Patsy adored waking up and having her coffee on the deck overlooking the bay. She and Charlie had a ski boat for years, and they taught all the kids and grandkids to water ski. They had a small sailboat they named the Jason D, after grandson #1, Jason. They enjoyed having friends come over and stay with them at the beach.

After 35 years of marriage to Charlie, Patsy and Fred reconnected. Fred describes it this way:

> The first time I saw Patsianne was at a party at my house. She walked in with her date, looked at me and smiled. That smile is still in my heart and will remain there forever. We got engaged and I went to San Diego for active duty with the Navy. We wrote and phoned until one evening we had an argument. I don't remember why, but it escalated quickly, and she said "well, I'm taking the ring off." I thought, well, that's it, and started going ashore again.
>
> We were apart for 34 years until one day I got a letter from Pat Gedney. She said she and her husband were coming to California and would my wife and I like to meet for coffee. My wife said "no" and her husband, Charlie, decided to play golf, so Pat and I met, and quickly realized the "old flame" was still there. We decided to leave our spouses and get married. We actually got married in Reno, Nevada, in a little chapel about a month before our "wedding" and didn't tell the family that we were already hitched. Our official wedding was on July 14, 1991, Bastille Day, and also her dad's birthday.

Telling the Story

We were married for 29 years until the Coronavirus came along. She put up a great fight, but when it started affecting her breathing, she couldn't keep up with it. She died on her 87th birthday.

Rest in peace, darlin'. I love you, Fred.

So, they came together after all those years apart. The love they shared as teenagers was rekindled, and they were "officially" married on Treasure Island, California. They remained in California for 10 years.

However, Patsy was missing her kids and grandkids who all lived on the East Coast. So, in 1999, they moved back East and bought a beautiful home in Newport News, Virginia. There they would gather with family to enjoy time together for nearly 20 more years. Patsy made many lifelong friends, including Betty Jane, and Skip, and John and Christi, as well as Lisa and Ken and their daughter Carol Ann, and also Gail. Patsy was a devoted mother, grandmother, great-grandmother. Every time she would talk about her family, her face would light up.

Many of her family and friends wrote tributes to Patsy after she died. Shannon Gedney shared about visiting her Grandma Pat and Aunt Chrissy in Arizona the summer of 2019. They were having a day in Aunt Chrissy's pool, just hanging out, the girls in the water, Fred and Shannon's boyfriend Ben sitting in the shade, chatting away. When Grandma Pat got out of the water, she wrapped herself in a towel, sat down on the couch, pulled out her compact mirror and lipstick, and started reapplying. Shannon said there was never a day that she saw her Grandma Pat not wearing lipstick, even after getting out of the pool. It was one of those "Yep, *that* is my grandmother!" moments. Grandma Pat wanted to look her best, no matter where she was or what she was doing. As they sat down for lunch, Grandma Pat said to Shannon, "I'm so glad to see you. You are so beautiful." Shannon said that Grandma Pat liked to nitpick at her when she was younger, so that turned into one of her favorite moments with her grandma.

Patsy's cousin Doris Reynolds remembers when Patsy brought Charlie over to their house to formally introduce him to their grandmother and her parents. Being a child, Doris was excited that her cousin was engaged. She remembers many fun times at Patsy's parents' house when they were all in the pool. Patsy's kids were all terrific swimmers. When Doris and her mother, Patsy's Aunt Isabel, would visit Leslie and Pete in Maryland, Patsy would try to come while they were there so they could all be together. Family was important to Patsy.

Patsy's nephew Shane Parreco remembers a series of Christmas ornaments that she gave him each year as his Christmas present. He also remembers times at her place in Rehoboth Beach. Shane said Patsy always spoke her mind and let you know if she thought you might be making a mistake. But Shane appreciated that about her. She said her piece, and it was up to the rest of them to figure out how to take it.

Patsy's niece Staci Cosby also remembers going to the beach house in Rehoboth, going on the boat, water skiing, going to the boardwalk. Staci remembers how Aunt Patsy came to see her kids after they were born. Staci also has fond memories of trips with Aunt Patsy like skiing and New York City. Staci will always remember Aunt Patsy for her big smile. (A lot of other people said that too—her beautiful smile).

Teresa Milano remembers her Aunt Patsy for her smile that lit up the room, and for her sense of adventure and willingness to learn new things. Theresa said the lengths she would go to support those she loved was unparalleled.

Her love of art and sense of beauty was deep. Joanne Wenger remembers when her Aunt Pat and Uncle Fred came for a visit when her son John was about 14 years old. John was a budding composer, and Pat showed particular excitement as they descended the basement steps to John's music room. Both Fred and Pat were taken with John's composition, but Pat could not stop complimenting John. She kept saying she was expecting something good, but she never expected "that!" A day later, Fred and Pat called to say that they wanted to give him $100, to use towards his music education. Four years later, John won the Maryland Distinguished Fine Arts Scholarship for composing. Joanne thanks Pat for smiling at John that day with her whole being.

Betty Jane Weigand said that she and Pat were like sisters. They were friends since grammar school. Her most fun memory is the two of them playing Monopoly every day one summer on her front porch when they were like 11. Pat was good at it and won a lot. Betty Jane says it is amazing when she thinks about it that they knew each other for all those years.

Several other friends shared memories on the obituary web site, and I encourage you to read them. But I want to share one more remembrance from Tom Andrews, who was Patsy's pastor for the past 16 years. Tom wrote, "Always stylish and classy, Patsy seemed at ease with people of higher social circles, but easily made friends with people who struggled and just barely got by." Tom said that he and his wife Ann always enjoyed their outings with Fred and Patsy. He said Patsy was "genuine and real, open and open-hearted. If you were her friend, you felt freely accepted. If you lacked honesty or integrity, Patsy could let her feelings be known too." Tom remembers a Tenebrae Good Friday service at their church. The service concluded with a surprise

Telling the Story

slamming of a door, which symbolized the closing of the tomb. Well, Patsy was there, and she was sitting directly in front of the door that was suddenly slammed shut. The stillness was broken as Patsy cried out when the door was closed, almost as if she had seen a ghost. But now, Tom said, as Patsy has passed over to the other side herself, what she sees is the resurrected Jesus, as her faith gives way to sight.

Chris shared with me a letter that Patsy sent to her dad back in 1992, not long before he passed. Patsy wrote:

> Dear Dad,
> I went to Mass yesterday at St. Mary's Cathedral in San Francisco, and we sang a hymn I'd heard before—and it really touched me. I wanted to write the words for you:
>
> You shall cross the barren desert
> But you shall not die of thirst
> You shall wander far in safety
> Though you do not know the way
> You shall speak your words in foreign lands
> And all will understand
> You shall see the face of God and live.
> ....
> If you pass through raging waters in the sea
> You shall not drown
> If you walk amid the burning flames
> You shall not be burned
> If you stand before the power of hell
> And death is at your side
> Know that I am with you through it all.
>
> Be not afraid
> I go before you always
> Come follow me
> And I will give you rest.
> ("Be Not Afraid," John Michael Talbot)

Patricia Anne Short Gedney West died on her birthday, December 20, 2020. Yes, it was her birthday, her birthday into new life with God. There is a passage in the Bible, 1 Peter 1:3-4, which says, "Blessed be the God and Father of our Lord Jesus Christ! By his great mercy he has given us a new birth into a living hope through the resurrection of Jesus Christ from the dead, and into an inheritance that is ... kept in heaven for you." Yes, Patsy has received her inheritance. She has been given "a new birth into a living hope through the resurrection of Jesus Christ from the dead."

Reflections

The memorial service for Patsy West was the second virtual eulogy I gave during the pandemic for a person who had died of COVID-19. One advantage of virtual services is that people can participate from many locations. Patsy's daughter, Chris, coordinated the service from her home in Arizona, and I gave the eulogy from my home in Maryland. The service included a video Chris had contracted, featuring many photos of her mother with family members and friends, set to inspirational music. It also included scripture readings, a poem, personal remembrances spoken by Patsy's sister Leslie and by Chris, and the eulogy and closing prayer.

I based the eulogy on a timeline Chris had provided of her mother's life; an email Patsy had sent me following the death of her first husband; and contributions from Patsy's other daughter, Patsy's husband, a granddaughter, a cousin, a nephew, three nieces, a lifelong friend, and her former pastor. Some of these contributions came in the form of emails sent directly to me or via Chris, while others came from entries on the funeral home's obituary web site.

For about two weeks before the memorial service, I received emails almost every day, in addition to occasional phone calls. There was even a virtual "dress rehearsal" to make sure the Zoom link worked, and that the order of service was doable. Chris did a masterful job of coordinating the many disparate elements and speakers. Following the service, "attendees" were invited to hang around in the meeting space to visit with each other.

Including contributions from so many people during the eulogy provided insights into Patsy's life from many different perspectives. Doing so, however, made the eulogy longer than usual. But no one seemed to mind that the service lasted more than an hour. In fact, I received feedback from several family members and friends that they appreciated hearing about Patsy from so many points of view.

Chapter 3
Lifting Up Our Christian Hope

The heart of our Christian hope is the affirmation of life after death. We who believe in Jesus believe that this life is not all there is; that this world is not all there is. We believe in heaven. We believe in life after death. We believe in eternal life. We believe that after our physical bodies die, our spiritual bodies are raised to new life with God. In my book, *Spelunking Scripture: Easter*, I begin the Introduction with this declaration: The resurrection of Jesus is the linchpin of the Christian faith. As Paul wrote:

> If Christ hasn't been raised, then your faith is worthless. (1 Cor. 15:17a, CEB)

But since Christ has been raised, all those who believe in him will be raised too.

In every eulogy I seek to lift up our Christian hope. It is not enough to give voice to our grief and to tell the story of the person who has died. As Christians, we have hope in the face of loss, hope that those who die in the Lord will live in the Lord. As Paul wrote, "If we live, we live to the Lord; and if we die, we die to the Lord; so then, whether we live, or whether we die, we are the Lord's" (Rom. 14:8). Jesus said, "I am the resurrection and the life. Those who believe in me, even though they die, will live, and everyone who lives and believes in me will never die" (John 11:25-26). Of course, we are mortal; but as Paul said, "the dead will be raised imperishable...this perishable body must put on imperishability, and this mortal body must put on immortality" (1 Cor. 15:52-53).

I have been blessed to know many people who lived with the hope of heaven in their hearts. One of those saints was Jo Reiter, the longtime pianist at my former church and one of mine and Linda's best friends. Years before she died, Jo gave me a folder containing instructions for her funeral. She had chosen the music, the scripture readings, and even listed suggestions for who might participate. From time to time, for several years after that, Jo would amend her instructions, even giving me some do's and don'ts to consider. She was always tactful, realizing that in the end her funeral was out of her control. But she wanted to give me some help, and to let me know that she was prepared when the time came for her to go. Jo was prepared because she lifted up our Christian hope by the way she lived.

Jo declined in health after I retired. Her daughters sent us word when it seemed the end was near, and Linda and I went to see her one last time in the nursing home. She was not responsive, but we talked to her, touched her, prayed over her, and told her we loved her. Somehow, I believe she knew we were there. Two of her daughters were there, and we spoke with them outside Jo's room before we left. Jo died the next day.

Eulogy for Jo Reiter
December 6, 2019

Jo Vanda Boyce Reiter was born on May 6, 1929. She was the daughter of Victor and Aurilla Boyce, and the sister of Victor James Boyce Jr.

Jo grew up in Norfolk, Virginia (or "Naah-fak" as she said it). She played softball, she loved to go out dancing with her friends, she loved music, and she loved to sing. Jo learned to play the piano as a child. During World War II, at a young age, Jo worked as a switchboard operator. She graduated from Granby High School in Norfolk in 1947. For two years she attended William and Mary College. Jo loved the water, and she spent a lot of time as a young adult on the beach at Virginia Beach with her friends. Her love of the water continued to the very end of her life. She appreciated just being able to look at the water, be it the ocean, bay, river, whenever she could.

When Jo was 23, she went to Sanford, Florida to stay with her beloved Uncle Ruby and Aunt Gladys. It was at Sanford that Jo met her future husband, Walter H. Reiter Jr. from Tom's River, New Jersey, who was stationed there in the Navy. Jo married Walt on December 19, 1953. After the wedding Jo lived in Ocean Gate, New Jersey with Walt's parents while he was in the Navy. After the Navy, Walt's subsequent jobs as a salesman caused them to live in a number of different locations, including Pittsburgh, Pennsylvania; Wheeling, West Virginia; and College Park, Maryland. Jo and Walt had five children: Jim, Linda Jo, Lee Ann, Karen, and Scott. The family moved to Bowie in 1966, and Jo lived here until 2012. Sadly, she and Walt divorced in 1975.

Jo was an avid gardener, and her family still enjoys seeing the dogwoods, azaleas, and other beautiful trees, plants, and flowers that she planted. Linda Jo and her family now live in the Bowie home. Jo was an avid reader and especially enjoyed reading about history. She kept up with politics and current affairs right until the end. Jo had a very sharp and learned mind. Jo was also an awesome cook! Southern food was her specialty. Not many kids in Bowie grew up eating and loving grits, but Jo's kids did! Her kids had to "undo" their Southern accents when they started school and learned that people here pronounce it "house" and not "hosse" (rhymes with "most," sort of).

Jo continued her love of athletics by playing volleyball. She continued her love of singing by joining the Sweet Adelines. She was the pianist here at Village Baptist Church, and she also played for funerals, weddings, and children's plays. Jo worked at the main office of the Duron Paint Company as a telecommunications coordinator from 1974 until her retirement in 1995. She continued friendships from her time there at Duron. She and her Duron friends shared many special outings together, including crab feasts and attending the Sugarloaf craft festivals. Never lacking in energy, after her retirement Jo continued working part-time as a receptionist at the Bowie Hearing Center.

Jo was fiercely independent. After she sold her Bowie home to Linda Jo, she lived in the small but tidy two-bedroom house in Edgewater from 2012 to 2017. Jo was able to continue to live there independently, thanks to the watchful care of her children and grandchildren. When she finally required some additional living assistance, she moved to the Annapolitan Assisted Living in 2017. Jo completely captured the hearts of the staff who cared for her there.

Much of what I've shared thus far was written by her family. Now, I want to focus my own words of appreciation on her many roles at Village Baptist Church. First, Jo was a charter member of Village Baptist Church. When the church was constituted back in 1971, Jo, her husband Walt, and four of their children were among the original members. Jo and her family actually came to this church before 1971, when Village was a mission of another church here in Bowie. So, Jo was active in this church almost from the very beginning.

Second, Jo was a pianist. Although she was not the primary church pianist in the early years, it wasn't long before Jo began to put her piano talents into service. By 1978, Jo was serving as *the* church pianist, playing for worship every Sunday morning and accompanying the choir in their weekly rehearsals. Jo continued as the every-week church pianist from 1978 until 1992, and she continued to play the piano after 1992 when her successor Linda Smith was away, and for special services such as Thanksgiving. Jo was an excellent pianist. Not only did she get the notes right: she played with such feeling and expression and beauty.

Third, Jo was a deacon. 1978, the year that Jo became the every-Sunday church pianist, was also the year that Jo was elected a deacon of Village Baptist Church. She was the first female to be elected as a deacon of the

Village church. And what a deacon she was! Jo was so dedicated in her service to the church family that she was elected to be a deacon nine times—in 1978, 1986, 1990, 1994, 1998, 2003, 2007, 2008, and 2012. Jo had a heart for helping others. When a young lady in our church who worked for the Census Bureau needed a place to live, Jo invited her to come live in her home. Mai Weismantle lived with Jo from 1997 until 2001. Of course, Mai paid rent, but for Jo it was about more than the money; it was about helping a young woman have a home. Jo extended her hospitality to many others. One Sunday we invited our former interim pastor James Dunn to come back to Village to preach, and his wife Marilyn to sing a solo. After the worship service that day, Jo invited James and Marilyn to come over to her house for lunch. Linda and I were blessed to be invited guests that day, too.

Fourth, Jo was a poet. Not only was Jo a charter member, and a church pianist, and a deacon, she also had a way with words. I don't remember exactly when it started, but every year Jo would write an original poem and read it for our annual Thanksgiving Day worship service here at the church. When we celebrated the church's 20th anniversary in 1991 on Homecoming Sunday, Jo wrote an original poem for that occasion. I can't read it like she did, but permit me to share part of what she wrote for that special occasion.

> Anniversary! What a wonderful word.
> Homecoming! Oh, the memories stirred.
> To you, who every Sunday are here,
> And you, who can only on visits appear,
> A handshake, a hug, and a "how-de-do"
> From each to every other in view.
> As we celebrate the church's 20th year,
> We think a bit and it's very clear
> That it didn't just happen this Village, ah no –
> It took planning and doing and guidance, and so
> Look back a bit and remember just how
> We walked the path from then to now.

Fifth, Jo was a role model. Jo had so many talents and gifts that she shared, as a charter member, and as a deacon, and as a pianist, and as a poet; but I think the biggest impact that Jo made for the people of this church was the way she lived out her Christian faith. People really looked up to Jo; they respected her; they admired her. Jo would have blushed if I had said that to her face, but she really did make an impact on people. Belinda Franklyn said, "She was a very sweet, caring soul." Cecelia Kurtz said, "In the words of my grandmother, she would be described as a grand lady and incredibly

Lifting Up Our Christian Hope

sweet." When Denise and Gary Miles' daughter was born a few years ago, they named her Avery Jo Miles. The "Jo" part of her name was in tribute to Jo Reiter. [I've since learned that Kira Jo Thompson Jackson also was named after Jo Reiter.] Now, Dan Ivins was pastor of Village for 10 years, and I served as pastor of Village for 33 years, but I don't know of any child that was named after Dan or named after me!

Kasey Malatesta called Jo "a beautiful soul." Jo's soul was beautiful, but not because she had an easy life. In fact, Jo's life was not easy. As Angela Sweetin put it, "Jo had more than her share of bumps and bruises along the way." Jo endured many troubles and heartaches, and yet, through her strong faith in Christ, Jo learned to endure and to overcome. A journalist once noticed that Fred Rogers, the children's TV star who sang about a "beautiful day in the neighborhood," would often ask people who were disabled or otherwise challenged to pray for him. The journalist asked Mr. Rogers, "Do you do that because you want to make them feel good?" Mr. Rogers replied, "Not at all. I just feel that people who have gone through as much as they have are very close to God." Jo Reiter went through a lot in her life. She would have considered it audacious to say it, but going through what she went through drew her close to God.

Jo had many passions in life: music, the world of nature, learning, being with her friends. But her greatest passions were her love for her family, and her love for her church family, and her love for God. The scripture from Titus that Jo selected to be read at her memorial service could very well be a theme verse for her life. Paul instructed Titus (and us) "to live lives that are self-controlled, upright, and godly...zealous for good deeds" (Titus 2:11, 14). That was Jo: self-controlled, upright, and godly, zealous for good deeds. In fact, Jo was so self-controlled that back in 2011 she started giving me specific instructions for her memorial service, and she continued to give me additional specific instructions in the years since then. Jo once told me, "When I die, just say, 'she died.' No euphemisms. That's country. Just say it!" OK—Jo died. I said it. Jo died, but that's not the end of Jo. She lives on in our hearts, and she lives eternally in the heart of God. So, we don't worry about Jo. She is with her Father in heaven. That is our Christian hope. Death is not the end of life. Jo has gone from us, but she is at home with God.

It was 17 years ago this week, back on December 1, 2002, that we dedicated the rebuilt church building. Some of you remember that the original church building was destroyed by fire in January of 2000, and it took 34 months to rebuild. I remember Jo was with us in the parking lot one day during the rebuilding as we watched a large construction crane lift the new steeple onto the roof of the rebuilt church. We didn't know whether to cheer or to cry. And finally, on that December day 17 years ago when we dedicated this rebuilt church, Jo played preludial music on that piano as the dedication service began. Linda Smith played a beautiful piano tribute during the service, but Jo also played the piano that day, and another of our charter members, Martha Potter, sang a solo. The dedication service was both a time to remember the past, and to look to the future. On the back of the dedication service program there was a hymn text titled, "For Builders Bold," by Herman Stuempfle. The hymn is about building a church, and that's what Jo Reiter helped to do: Jo helped to build not just the physical structure, but the church as the body of Christ and the people of God. The hymn begins:

> For builders bold, whose vision pure
> Saw more than bricks or stone,
> Who laid in hope foundations sure
> With Christ the cornerstone;
> For those who honored your commands
> And trusted your strong Word,
> Who offered faithful hearts and hands,
> We give you thanks, O Lord.

And then the hymn concludes with this stanza:

> We come, O Lord, inheritors
> From those whose work is done.
> Lord, make us now contributors
> To years beyond our own.
> Let faith's enkindled flame not fail;
> Let love's best gifts increase.
> Let hope in Christ's sure Word prevail
> Till heart and time shall cease.

I'm not a poet like Herman Stuempfle was, or like Jo Reiter was, but here's how I would put it:

> The bench is empty
> The pianist is gone
> Our hearts are heavy
> But the melody lingers on,
> The melody lingers on.

Reflections

Lifting up our Christian hope can be done in two ways: through the words of Holy Scripture, and through the holy life of a person such as Jo Reiter. To say that Jo lived a holy life is not to say she was perfect. None of us are. But Jo lived a life dedicated to God, and the hope of her faith in Christ shined through her. Jo did not live an easy life, but she lived a blessed life.

Our Christian hope is for life after death, to be sure. But it is also about life in this world, life that prevails in struggle, life that is joyful even after heartbreak. Jo lived that kind of life. I am not talking platitudes here. Jo struggled.

She struggled emotionally after her husband left her for another woman. She struggled financially to provide for her children and to take care of her own needs. She struggled to support her children after they were grown and faced their own life challenges. But because the hope of Christ was in her heart, Jo was able to endure the struggles of life and overcome. She lifted up her Christian hope by the way the she lived.

The latest version of Jo's instructions for her memorial service were dated 9/10/17. That was when she was still living independently, more than two years before Jo died. She wrote to her family (and to me):

> Memorial Service at Village <u>**NO ASHES AT MEMORIAL SERVICE**</u> !!! No visitation necessary—or wanted. VBC will likely offer a "repast" after Memorial Service. If so, have just finger foods so people can move around and visit—no sit-down meal. Bruce will guide you all in arranging a simple memorial service.

There also were instructions about music, scripture readings, scripture readers, and who would sing a solo ("whatever she chooses to sing will be <u>exactly</u> what I want"). She also wrote:

> During the service, <u>**DO NOT THROW OPEN THE FLOOR**</u> by saying, "If there is anyone who would like to say a few words..." etc. I find that extremely awkward and want <u>no part</u> of it for me. Only 1 or 2 pictures, snapshots, <u>if</u> you want them, displayed. Nothing more—if nothing, that's fine, also. Any obituary notice should be simple, basic information.

Jo knew that her memorial service would be about her, but she sought to guide her family (and me) to make it as unpretentious as possible. She wanted the focus to be on each other, and on our Christian hope.

Chapter 4
Gone Too Soon

After I retired, Linda and I were in South Bend, Indiana visiting our friends Leslie and Roger Alford when I received a call from Mark Miles, a friend from our former church. I could tell from the tone in his voice that something was wrong. Finally, Mark said, "Bodhi is gone." What!?! Bodhi was Mark and Michele's grandson, the second son of their daughter Audry. He was only five months old.

What happened? Mark could not say for sure. Audry had gone with Michele to Alabama for Michele's mother's memorial service. She had left Bodhi and his big brother Miles with their father, Nick. Nick had taken the boys to visit his parents a couple of hours away, near Ocean City, Maryland. Nick and the two boys had gone for a stroll on the boardwalk, with Bodhi in his stroller. Then Nick had put the two boys in their car seats and driven to a restaurant to meet up with his parents. He took the older boy Miles into the restaurant first, then came back to the car to get Bodhi. The baby was still in his car seat, but he was not moving. Nick ran back into the restaurant and called for help. A paramedic who was eating in the restaurant rushed out to the car to help. They called for an ambulance. Bodhi was taken to the hospital. But it was too late: Bodhi was gone.

I had to sit down while Mark was telling me the story. It was just too painful to take standing up. I had known Audry almost her entire life. I had baptized her. I had officiated their wedding when she and Nick got married. I had dedicated Miles when he was a baby. I would have dedicated Bodhi too, but by the time he was born, I had retired from the church. Now, Bodhi was gone, and the family wanted me to know. They wanted me to officiate at his memorial service. They were not sure when it would be, but they could wait until I got back in town.

Linda and I were planning to drive up to Grand Rapids, Michigan the next day, and then to fly back to Maryland the day after that. While we were waiting for our flight at the Grand Rapids airport, I talked with Mark again. We settled on a date for the memorial service at the church. Then I started making phone calls to recruit participants for the service. The regular church organist was not available, but the substitute organist could play. I called one of the regular soloists in the church to see if she could sing. She said she could. I called the co-chairs of the hospitality committee to see if they could arrange a repast for after the service. They said they could. I called the church secretary to alert her to the arrangements and to ask her to be ready to prepare the printed program for the service after I got back. I called Mark again to tell him about the arrangements I had made. I told him I would come to see Audry and Nick the next day. Then I began to think: What would I say? What would I say to Audry and Nick when I saw them? And what would I say during the eulogy for Bodhi's memorial service? He was gone far too soon.

The day after we returned to Maryland, I went to Mark and Michele's house to see Audry and Nick. They were staying there with their son Miles. It was just too painful for them to go home without Bodhi. It turned out that I did not have to say much. I sat with Audry and Nick and heard about what had happened. Then I asked them to tell me about Bodhi. I took notes as they told the story of Bodhi's life. Audry told me she would sing "You Are My Sunshine" as she rocked Bodhi to sleep. It broke my heart to see their broken hearts. I went downstairs to see Miles playing with Michele and Mark. Miles was too young to fully understand what had happened, but he knew that Bodhi was gone.

At the memorial service we sang the hymn, "Children Are a Gift from Heaven." We read scripture, and Kasey, the soloist, sang "Baby Mine." Members of the family, including Mark and Bodhi's other grandfather, shared personal remembrances. The organist, Jeannine, played "You Are My Sunshine" on the piano. Then I gave the eulogy, in three parts: Remembering Bodhi, Coming to Grips with Our Loss, and Claiming Our Christian Hope. The sound technician, Dave, played a recording of "Over the Rainbow" by Iz to end the service. Then we moved from the sanctuary into the fellowship hall for a repast. The family had written this obituary for the back of the printed program:

> Our sweet Bodhi Shepard Paska, or as we called him, Bodhi Bear, passed away suddenly after five short, but full months with us. He was a tough guy that could teach us all about resilience. While Bodhi spent his first month in the NICU at Johns Hopkins, he then came home to a summer full of adventures. Bodhi spent his time with family and friends building memories at Smith Mountain Lake, Deep Creek Lake, camping, several boat rides, many trips to parks and the beach. Bodhi loved kisses on his cheeks and lit up every time his big brother Miles was nearby. He started chatting just to make sure he kept up with Miles. Bodhi had an extra big smile, or as Miles liked to say, his "Googoo Gaga Face." Bodhi will forever be loved and cherished by all those who met him. He leaves behind a large family who

Gone Too Soon

will hold him in their hearts. In lieu of flowers, please make a donation to Project Sweet Peas to help other families navigate through NICU stays and the loss of a baby.

A Celebration of Life in Loving Memory of Bodhi Shephard Paska
October 10, 2019
Village Baptist Church, Bowie, Maryland

Prelude Jeannine Case

Call to Worship and Invocation Bruce Salmon

On behalf of the family, we welcome you to this celebration of life in loving memory of Bodhi Paska. We gather here today to remember Bodhi, to celebrate his life, to give thanks to God for the time we had with him, and to comfort one another in our loss. With the sure conviction that God is here, let us turn to the Father in prayer:

> Our Father in Heaven,
> we have gathered in this time of sadness, and celebration, to reaffirm our faith in you, to place our hearts within the shelter of your loving care. We have gathered to say goodbye to this beloved son, and brother, and grandson, and nephew, and cousin, but also to seek your consolation as we deal with our sorrow and come to grips with our loss. As we mourn, help us to mourn in hope, knowing that Jesus has prepared a place for Bodhi, that Jesus is with us even now, and that Jesus will be with us in every experience of life. Give us, O God, a new awareness of your presence in our midst. Give us the grace to remember with gratitude, and to look to the future with hope, in the sure and certain promise of eternal life. This we pray in the name of Jesus, who rose victorious from the dead, and who lives forevermore that we might live victorious with you. Amen.

*Hymn "Children Are a Gift from Heaven" # 685

Hear now these words from Holy Scripture:

> People were bringing little children to him in order that he might touch them; and the disciples spoke sternly to them. But when Jesus saw this, he was indignant and said to them, "Let the little children come to me; do not stop them; for it is to such as these that the kingdom of God belongs. Truly I tell you, whoever does not receive the kingdom of God as a little child will never enter it." And he took them up in his arms, laid his hands on them, and blessed them. (Mark 10:13-16)

God is our refuge and strength, a very present help in trouble. Therefore we will not fear, though the earth should change, though the mountains shake in the heart of the sea… There is a river whose streams make glad the city of God, the holy habitation of the Most High. God is in the midst of the city; it shall not be moved. God will help it when the morning dawns. The Lord of hosts is with us; the God of Jacob is our refuge. (Ps. 46:1-5, 7)

My soul is bereft of peace; I have forgotten what happiness is; so I say, "Gone is my glory, and all that I had hoped for from the Lord." But this I call to mind, and therefore I have hope: The steadfast love of the Lord never ceases, his mercies never come to an end; they are new every morning; great is your faithfulness. "The Lord is my portion," says my soul, "therefore I will hope in him." The Lord is good to those who wait for him, to the soul that seeks him. It is good that one should wait quietly for the salvation of the Lord. (Lam. 3:17, 26)

Do not let your hearts be troubled. Believe in God, believe also in me. In my Father's house there are many dwelling places. If it were not so, would I have told you that I go to prepare a place for you? And if I go and prepare a place for you, I will come again and will take you to myself, so that where I am, there you may be also. (John 14:1-4)

Listen, I will tell you a mystery! We will not all die, but we will all be changed, in a moment, in the twinkling of an eye, at the last trumpet. For the trumpet will sound, and the dead will be raised imperishable, and we will be changed. For this perishable body must put on imperishability, and this mortal body must put on immortality. When this perishable body puts on imperishability, and this mortal body puts on immortality, then the saying that is written will be fulfilled: "Death has been swallowed up in victory. Where, O death, is your victory? Where, O death, is your sting?" The sting of death is sin, and the power of sin is the law. But thanks be to God, who gives us the victory through our Lord Jesus Christ. (1 Cor. 15:51-57)

If we live, we live to the Lord; and if we die, we die to the Lord; so then, whether we live, or whether we die, we are the Lord's. (Rom. 14:8)

This is the Word of the Lord—thanks be to God.

Solo	"Baby Mine" *by Washington & Churchill*	Kasey Malatesta

Gone Too Soon

Personal Remembrances
Some of you may wish to share a brief, personal remembrance about Bodhi. We invite you to raise your hand that I might recognize you, then come to the pulpit and speak into the microphone, expressing your words of remembrance and appreciation.

Piano Tribute	"You Are My Sunshine"	Jeannine Case
Eulogy		Bruce Salmon

Remembering Bodhi

Bodhi Shepard Paska was born on May 1, 2019, at 5:31 p.m. at Anne Arundel Medical Center in Annapolis, Maryland. He was the second child of Audry and Nick Paska, the younger brother of Miles Paska.

Bodhi was loved from the moment he was born. Yet, his health was precarious from the very beginning. The next day Bodhi was transferred to Johns Hopkins Hospital in Baltimore where he would have surgery, less than 48 hours after his birth. After the surgery, Bodhi was placed in the Neonatal Intensive Care Unit, NICU, where he would be treated for almost a month. Despite being only 6 lbs., 14 oz. at birth, Bodhi was a fighter. He was a strong baby who overcame a very difficult start to his life. For almost the first two weeks of his life, Bodhi couldn't eat. He was sustained by IVs. But then, on May 14, Bodhi started eating. What a day!

Bodhi was able to come home, for the first time, on May 29, 2019. It was a joyous homecoming for the entire family. I have a photo on my phone that Bodhi's Pop Pop, Mark Miles, sent me the following week, on June 8. It's a photo of the proud grandfather Mark holding his grandson, just over six weeks old. It was obvious that Bodhi was cherished. Yet, Bodhi's medical issues were not over. On June 14, Bodhi underwent another surgery at Johns Hopkins; it was just eight weeks after the first surgery. Yet, after an overnight stay, Bodhi was able to come home and rejoin his family.

Barely two weeks after that second surgery, Bodhi went on his first family vacation, to Smith Mountain Lake. Almost the entire Miles side of the family was there. It was a vacation that had been planned the previous September, long before Bodhi was born. As I said, almost the entire Miles family was there the last week in June. Everyone got to know Bodhi, and he got to know them. Bodhi even went on his first boat ride on the Lake. But the summer adventures were far from over. Back in Maryland, Bodhi visited the National Aquarium in Baltimore. He went to Deep Creek Lake with his parents and his brother, where he met some of their friends who had served with them in Hawaii. Bodhi took another boat ride. Bodhi also went on a camping trip with his family and the Kirk family to a site along the C&O Canal in western Maryland. Bodhi spent a week at Massanutten with his Miles grandparents, along with his Uncle Gary and Aunt Denise and cousins, Jordan and Avery Jo. Bodhi also visited his grandparents on the Paska side of the family at the beach in Delaware.

Bodhi crammed a lot into his life in the months after his second surgery in June. Then, on September 25, Bodhi had a third surgery at Johns Hopkins. Again, it was only an overnight stay, and he did well. He was doing so well that last week his mother left Bodhi and Miles with their father Nick so she could go to Alabama to attend the memorial service for her grandmother, Beth. That's just the way Bodhi was: he did well, even though he went through some tough times medically. Audry said that Bodhi was "the hardest easy baby ever." By that she meant that in spite of his medical issues, Bodhi did well. He was a good sleeper. They would put him to bed, and from midnight to 5 or 6 or even 7 in the morning he would sleep.

When he wasn't sleeping, Bodhi was a joy to be around. His brother Miles was crazy about him. The two boys just liked hanging out together. Bodhi would look around and smile, and even say some things, although no one knew exactly what he was saying. He was "the hardest easy baby ever."

Coming to Grips with Our Loss

How then do we sum up Bodhi's life? Needless to say, it was a life that ended far too soon. Yet, Bodhi lived a good life! Bodhi was loved; he was surrounded by love. Indeed, Bodhi is loved even now. The challenge for us is finding the strength to carry on. Those who knew Bodhi and loved Bodhi are not going to get over this. Those who knew and loved Bodhi will be forever changed by his life and by his passing. The question is: What kind of change will we experience? Will this experience make us angry or bitter or despairing? Or will this experience make us kinder and more compassionate and more loving and more appreciative of life?

Claiming Our Christian Hope

This we know: We don't have to worry about Bodhi. He is with his Father in heaven. Jesus had a special place in his heart for little children—he took them in his arms and blessed them. The One who knew and loved Bodhi before he was even born is the same God who is holding Bodhi close to his heart now and forever. That is our Christian hope. Death is not the end of life. Bodhi has gone from us, but he is at home with God.

Dear Father of the Risen Christ,
With you, there is no death. Our beloved Bodhi has gone from us but is at home with you. And so, our Father, we don't worry about Bodhi. We know he is in your joyous presence. The journey of his life on earth has ended, and he has now entered eternal life with you. Help us, O God, to move through this time of sadness. Help us not to forget him, but to learn to live without him. Help us to cherish his memory, but to find the faith and strength to carry on.

We pray especially for Audry, for Nick, for Miles, for his grandparents and for other family members. Help them to find the strength to carry on.

Strengthen us, our Father, as we face some lonely days ahead. May the pain we feel yield to sweet remembrances of his time with us, and memories of a love that will never die. We trust in you, our loving Heavenly Father. Hold us close in your everlasting arms.

This we pray in Jesus' name, Amen.

"Over the Rainbow"
Iz

Reflections

Baptists do not baptize babies for several reasons: First, Baptists believe that baptism is for believers, persons who have made a voluntary profession of faith in Jesus and have chosen to be baptized as an expression of that faith. Second, Baptists believe that baptism is symbolic, not salvific. Baptism does not convey salvation; rather, it symbolizes the new life in Christ. Third, Baptists believe that until a person reaches the "age of accountability," that person is secure within God's loving care. Since babies are too young to make a faith decision, we believe that God welcomes them into his presence should they die. Of course, we believe that God holds all persons within his loving care, but God does not force faith on anyone.

When a baby dies, it is a tragedy, but it is not a theological crisis. We do not worry about the soul of the baby. We know where the baby is: The baby is with God. Losing a baby or a child is one of the most difficult experiences a parent can have, but we grieve for those who have been left behind, not for the child who is now in heaven. Still, the loss of a child is devastating.

The maternal grandparents of Bodhi Paska, Mark and Michele Miles, are two of our closest friends. We traveled with them to the Baptist World Congress in Birmingham, England in 2005. We took a trip together to southern Utah to visit the national parks there. They joined us for a trip to the Baptist World Congress in Durban, South Africa in 2015. Mark and I have taken more than a dozen golf trips together. So, when Mark called to say that Bodhi had died, he was calling me not just as his former pastor but as his friend.

Linda and I have known Audry, Bodhi's mother, since she was a toddler. They are almost like family to us. So, we shared in the devastation of losing Bodhi. But we did not worry about Bodhi's eternal destiny. We worried about those left behind—Bodhi's parents and grandparents and other family members and friends. My goal with the eulogy for Bodhi was to bring some comfort and closure to those who will never fully "get over" his death. The eulogy was a step in the journey that they will be on for the rest of their lives. It was not the end of the journey, but it was a step.

Chapter 5
Sudden Loss

It was Thanksgiving Day, 2002. We had gathered in our rebuilt sanctuary for our annual Thanksgiving worship service. After the church building had burned in January of 2000, our congregation had been displaced for 34 months while we rebuilt. Now, we were back home, and the reasons for our thanksgiving were multiplied. Joining us that day were two first-time visitors: a mother and her four-year-old daughter. They had heard about the church that had lost its building and was now back in its new facility, and they had come to worship with us. They returned to worship with us on Sunday, and they kept coming. Eventually, the mother and her husband joined our church, and they were baptized on the same day. Their names were Barbara and Richard Dashiell, and their daughter was Amelia Grace. They soon became integral parts of our church family.

In June of 2009, Linda and I were in Houston to attend the annual meeting of the Cooperative Baptist Fellowship. We had checked into our hotel on Tuesday and purchased our tickets for the Religious Liberty Luncheon of the Baptist Joint Committee. On Wednesday we were planning out our schedule for the day when we received a call from a deacon of our church. He had terrible news. Dashiell and his 10-year-old daughter Amelia had been killed in an auto accident. I called Barb to express our grief and our support. We cancelled our hotel reservations and changed our plane tickets to return to Maryland that night.

The next day, I met Barb and her sister at the funeral home. I offered to go with Barb into the back room to identify the bodies of Rick and Amelia. She said she preferred to see them alone. With incredible strength, she went by herself into the room. After a few moments, she came out, her eyes filled with tears, but with a resolve to carry on. We began to plan the memorial service for her husband and their only child.

I had not planned to be at church that Sunday. I had recruited a guest preacher to be there in my absence, while Linda and I visited my mother in Texas following the CBF General Assembly. But after our hasty return, I had called the guest preacher and explained what had happened. He graciously deferred, to allow me to share with the congregation that Sunday the tragic news.

During the Sunday School hour, the teacher of Amelia's class asked me to come to her classroom and speak with the class members. I told them what had happened and answered their questions as best I could. Some of the children cried. I felt like crying myself.

I had written that morning's sermon in less than three days, and I delivered it to the stunned congregation that Sunday morning. I was not expecting them to attend, but Barb, her sister, and her mother were there. After the service Barb told me that it was a hard sermon for them to hear, but they needed to be there with us. They would be with us again in church on the following Saturday for the memorial service. Below is the sermon I gave in church that Sunday after Rick and Amelia died.

Blessed Be the Name of the Lord
Job 1:13-21, 2:9-13
Village Baptist Church, Bowie, Maryland
July 5, 2009

As you know, five days ago, a family in our church suffered an unspeakable loss. Ten-year-old Amelia Dashiell was riding in a car driven by her father Rick Dashiell on I-70 in Howard County Tuesday night. Rick was behind the wheel of their classic 1929 Model A Ford, and Amelia was in the passenger seat. They were traveling in the far-right lane about 50-miles-an-hour around 6:30 p.m. when a man driving a 2007 Dodge struck their vehicle from behind. Their antique car was forced off the road and rolled over several times. Both Amelia and Rick were thrown from the vehicle and killed. The other driver was not injured.

About 9:30 p.m. that evening, state troopers came to the Dashiells' home to give Barb the terrible news. There is no way to be prepared for something like that. In an instant, the two most precious people in her life were gone.

Linda and I were in Houston Tuesday night to attend the General Assembly of the Cooperative Baptist Fellowship. On Wednesday morning there were messages on my cell phone from Pete Parreco and Ron Knode. After speaking with Ron, I was able to reach Barb on her cell phone and told her that we would catch the next flight available back to Maryland. We finally got out Wednesday night. On the three-hour flight back to BWI, I tried to think of something to say in the face of such a tragedy. I was thinking about what I might say at the funeral, and what I might say to you here in worship this morning. For three hours I thought, and I prayed, and I could not

Sudden Loss

come up with a thing. Actually, I came up with about a dozen beginnings to a funeral message, and several beginnings to a sermon, but none of them seemed right. So basically, I sat on the plane for three hours and came up with nothing. Sometimes silence is the only answer you are given in the face of such a crushing blow.

After I met with Barb on Thursday to discuss the memorial service for Rick and Amelia, I sat down to write this sermon. I did not have a particular text in mind until I thought about the biblical character of Job. You remember the story. Job was a man who seemingly had everything…a wife, seven sons and three daughters, "seven thousand sheep, three thousand camels, five hundred yoke of oxen, five hundred donkeys, and very many servants, so that he was the greatest of all the people of the east" (Job 1:3). Beyond all that, Job was a man of integrity, blameless and upright, one who feared God and turned away from evil. In other words, Job had everything a man could want. Then, in an instant, almost all was taken away.

Job's multiple losses were bad enough, but even harder was that it made no sense. Job lost almost everything, and it was not Job's fault. Job had done nothing wrong. Job was a good man who lived an upright and blameless life. Yet tragedy after tragedy befell him, and he lost almost everything.

I think the reason that the book of Job is in the Bible is because Job's experience is the human experience. Bad things happen, in every life, and sometimes the bad things that happen are not our fault.

During a storm, a branch fell from a tree on Connecticut Avenue, striking a passing minivan, killing a mother and her seven-year-old daughter inside, while five other children escaped serious injury. A Metro train on the Red Line operating in automatic mode failed to detect a stopped train ahead at the Fort Totten Station and crashed into it, killing eight passengers and the train operator. Random, irrational, nonsensical, bad things happen to good people.

It was not Rick and Amelia's fault that their vehicle was rear-ended on I-70 in Howard County Tuesday night. Rick was driving in the far-right lane at 50-miles-an-hour. He even had a "Slow Moving Vehicle" sticker on the rear window of his antique car. Of course, accidents happen on the highway every day, and tens of thousands of people lose their lives in traffic fatalities every year. But when it happens to someone we know, our hearts cry out. One message from the book of Job is that bad things happen, even when it's not our fault. We cannot explain it. It does not make any sense. That is simply the nature of life on this earth.

Last year my Pastor's Sunday School Class studied the book of Job. We read it verse by verse, chapter by chapter, almost the entire book. And as we read it, we kept asking, "Why?" Why did Job have to suffer like he did? We kept reading, looking for an answer. Near the end of the book, God finally spoke to Job. But when God spoke, he did not answer the question of human suffering. There are questions this side of heaven that seem to have no answer, except to say that is the nature of life on this earth. One message of Job is that bad things happen, and sometimes good people suffer.

But there is more to Job than that. Another message from Job is that while bad things happen, we need not go through suffering alone. When Job's friends heard of his troubles they rushed to his side. They came together to console and comfort him. Seeing him from a distance, they did not recognize him; Job was so distraught and overcome with grief. In sympathy with Job the friends wept aloud, and rent their clothes in mourning, and threw dust in the air upon their heads as an expression of their collective grief. Then they sat with Job on the ground for seven days and seven nights, and no one spoke a word. They sat in utter silence, for they saw that his grief was very great.

So, a second message from Job is that we need not go through suffering alone. I know that Barb has been surrounded by family members and friends these last few days. Our entire church feels a collective sense of loss. Just about every person I have spoken with about this tragedy has been broken up about it. I have tried to remain composed for Barb and her family and the members of our church who have been devastated by this loss, but there have been times when waves of grief have washed over me.

I was sitting at a traffic light and watched an antique car go by, and I felt my sunglasses fogging up. I woke up at 4:00 a.m. one morning, and felt my pillow wet with tears. Carlynn Thompson emailed me some pictures that she and Dave had taken of Amelia over the years at Vacation Bible School and other children's activities. I sat at my computer, and my eyes welled up as I looked at the photos of that beautiful little girl growing up. I read the story in the newspaper yesterday morning while eating breakfast about the mother and daughter who were killed by that falling tree branch on Connecticut Avenue, and I cried in my cereal. Many of you have been crying, too.

The message of Job is that we are in this together. When bad things happen, we need not cry alone, and we need not suffer alone. Sometimes all we can do is come together to console and comfort one another. Sometimes all we can do is to weep with those who weep. Sometimes there is nothing we can say, nothing we can do, but to sit together in silence. But there is power in sympathy, and power in presence. Job's friends certainly did not have all the answers. But their presence, their sympathy, their tears, their sitting together in silence with their friend, was a comfort and a consolation. When bad things happen to any of us, let us be there for one another.

The book of Job offers no easy answers in the face of senseless suffering. Instead, the book of Job offers the example of one who suffered and yet who did not give up. Job was pushed to the limits of human endurance, but he did not give up on God. His wife said to him, "Do you still persist in your integrity? Curse God and die." She advised Job to surrender to despair. But though he suffered terribly, Job would not give up on God. He remained faithful to God, even though he did not understand his suffering. He trusted God, even though his multiple losses of family and property and health made no sense. With incredible faith, Job prayed: "The Lord gave, and the Lord has taken away, blessed be the name of the Lord."

The message of Job is never give up on God, because God never gives up on us. Even in the midst of inexplicable suffering God is there. "I will never leave you or forsake you," Jesus said (Heb. 13:5). In Romans 8:26 Paul wrote, "Likewise the Spirit helps us in our weakness; for we do not know how to pray as we ought, but that very Spirit intercedes with sighs too deep for words." Paul continued in Romans 8:28: "We know that all things work together for good for those who love God." That does not mean that all things that happen are good. Some things that happen are very bad. But God works even in those bad things to bring good out of them. I do not know exactly what good can come out of this tragedy that has befallen Barb and her family, but I know that God is at work, even in this, because Jesus will never leave us or forsake us.

God knows the pain of a parent losing an only child. God knows that pain because he gave his only Son to die on a cross. The bread and the cup on this Lord's Supper table are signs of God's presence, signs of God's love for us. Even when the worst happens, we have hope. The Power that resurrected Jesus from the dead will raise up every soul who believes in him. Death is not the end of life. Through our faith in Jesus, death is but the gateway to new and greater and everlasting life with God.

In all things, in all things, in all things, blessed be the name of the Lord.

Memorial Service

The memorial service for Rick and Amelia Dashiell included a prelude and postlude by the church pianist, Linda Smith, and the former church pianist, Jo Reiter. The congregation sang the hymn "He Is Our Peace." There were scripture readings by family members and a duet by Amelia's uncle and the deacon who had called us with the news, Ron Knode. Another soloist from our church, Kasey Malatesta, sang "When I Get Where I'm Going." Then members of the congregation were invited to share personal remembrances.

After a slide presentation, I gave the eulogy. There was another solo by Ron Knode, "I Can Only Imagine." After the closing hymn, "Amazing Grace," there was a flag presentation by a United States Military Honor Guard. Following the benediction and postlude, the family received guests in the fellowship hall.

The back of the printed program contained an overview of Rick and Amelia's lives, written by the family.

Richard (Rick) Thomas Dashiell
Amelia Grace Dashiell

On June 30, 2009, the Lord Jesus finished the place He had prepared in heaven for Rick and Amelia Dashiell and called them to be there with Him forever. They were deeply loved and will be greatly missed by each and every person whose lives they touched.

Rick is survived by his wife of almost 13 years, Barbara Jeanne Dashiell, and 3 brothers, Louis, William, and James. He was the father of the late Amelia Grace Dashiell. Rick led a full and exciting life. He was a devoted husband and father and a good friend to his family and others he knew. Rick served 6 years in the Navy immediately following high school, and later traveled extensively making friends around the world too numerous to count. Rick was an excellent provider for his family and did so while employed at Washington Area Metro Transit Authority, and most recently with the District of Columbia Water and Sewer Authority. Rick loved the outdoors and working with his hands. You could say he was somewhat of a Renaissance man in his many pursuits. Rick was educated as a teacher, though his career path led him outside the classroom setting, he is remembered for his ability to mentor and teach so many people as his life touched theirs. You could always count on Rick being there to help you in your need. His death creates a major void in our lives.

Amelia is survived by her loving mother, Barbara Jeanne Dashiell, her grandmother, Jeanne Marie Benzel, and a host of loving aunts, uncles, relatives and friends. She was the daughter of the late Richard Thomas Dashiell. Amelia received her entire 6 years of education as a home schooler at The Homestead Academy. She was involved in many activities with our church, including singing with the Children's Choir and performing with the Youth Dance Ministry. Amelia completed 4 years of private piano lessons; she passed her grade 1 Cecchetti ballet student exam. Her true passion was horses and she fancied herself a cowgirl. She would rather be at the barn than anywhere else, happily exercising, grooming, training and spoiling the horses. She was a member of the Centaurs 4-H Horse Club and won several ribbons, trophies and awards, both on horseback and with her knowledge of horsemanship. Amelia was proud of her volunteer work with a local therapeutic riding program. In fact, Amelia loved animals in general and helped care for the family's many pets including chickens, goats, sheep, guinea pigs, a rabbit and dogs. However, Amelia's most outstanding attribute had to be her special gift of touching the hearts and lives of everyone she met. She was an especially compassionate, tenderhearted child with a sense of humor beyond her years. She is greatly missed.

Eulogy for Rick and Amelia Dashiell
Village Baptist Church, Bowie, Maryland
July 11, 2009

"The eternal God is your dwelling place, and underneath are the everlasting arms." (Deut. 33:27)

Dear Family and Friends,

We have gathered here today to remember Rick and Amelia Dashiell, to celebrate the gift of their lives, and to comfort one another in our loss. We have gathered to say goodbye to these ones we loved, but also to place our trust in God who is our dwelling place, and who will hold us in his everlasting arms. We have gathered to mourn, but as Christians we mourn in hope, knowing that Jesus has gone to prepare a place for us, and that Jesus is with us even now in this time of sorrow, and that Jesus will be with us in every experience of life. We have gathered because we need to be here, in the presence of one another, and in the presence of our Father in heaven. And so, this is a time when tears are allowed, and laughter too.

A couple of years ago, the Flower Committee was here on a Saturday morning decorating our church for the Christmas season. Amelia was here that day. Technically, Amelia was not on the Flower Committee, but she often came with her mother, or if her mother could not be here, she came with her Aunt Laura, whom her mother sometimes recruited to help decorate in her place. Last December, as I recall, Amelia and Laura did a lot of the decorating themselves, including hanging wreaths on the windows and helping with the Chrismon Tree. But this was the year before that, and Amelia was here, but she did not have any particular assignment.

I was helping out too, and I noticed that morning that wherever I went, Amelia was right behind me. I went to retrieve an Advent banner out of the back room that her mother had helped make, and Amelia was right there.

I carried a box of decorations into the sanctuary, and Amelia was close on my heels. I tracked down an extension cord, and Amelia was there. It wasn't that she was bothering me; in fact, she hardly said a word. She just watched what I was doing and followed my every step like my shadow. Finally, Amelia said, "Do you mind if I follow you?" I replied, "No, I don't mind at all, but I'm not doing anything very interesting." That did not seem to deter her, and she was by my side most of that morning.

I thought about that seemingly insignificant incident that happened a couple of years ago, and I came to realize this week that Amelia has still been following me—for the past 11 days and nights she has never been far from my thoughts, and she has been there even in my dreams.

I loved Amelia, as most of you did. I loved Rick, too, but not in the way that one loves a child. I remember the first time that I met her. She was barely four years old, still young enough to be carried in her mother's arms. Barb and Amelia were here on Thanksgiving Day, 2002, for our annual Thanksgiving worship service. Our church had recently been rebuilt after a devastating fire, and we were especially thankful that day to be back in our church home. Barb was visiting our church that day for the first time, with four-year-old Amelia. I remember them sitting on the right-hand side, near the windows. We would meet Rick shortly after that, but we met Barb and Amelia for the first time that day almost seven years ago.

Amelia was so shy that she would hardly let go of her mother. But for most of us, as far as Amelia was concerned, it was love at first sight. That beautiful, shy little girl soon found a place in our hearts, where she remains to this day. We literally watched Amelia grow up, right before our eyes. So, Barb, you are going to have to bear with us as we talk about our little girl.

She was yours first, and Rick's, of course, and her grandmother's, and she belonged to a host of uncles and aunts and godparents and friends. But she belonged to us, too, and we loved her. We shared your pride, as she grew from that shy little girl into a poised little lady, on the verge of becoming a young woman.

Amelia was everything that parents would want their daughter to be… she was loving, she was kind, she was faithful, she was true, she was smart, she was industrious, she was sincere. Amelia was a devoted daughter and granddaughter, and niece; she was a friend to many. Amelia was also a follower of Jesus Christ; she loved Jesus, and she earnestly sought to live according to his will. How could you not be proud, how could all of us not be proud of Amelia, and delight in her presence?

Yes, Amelia has been following me. Thank God, I can't get her out of mind, or out of my heart. Amelia Grace Dashiell was born on September 16,

1998, in Baltimore, Maryland. She was the only child of Richard and Barbara Dashiell. It was Rick who gave Amelia the middle name, Grace, because as he told Barb, "She is a gift from God."

At an early age Amelia developed a love for animals. She loved everything horses, and once told her mother, "I feel happiest when I'm riding." Her love for animals eventually found expression in a dog-washing business, a job exercising horses, and this spring she launched her own chicken farming business. She helped build the chicken coop, painted it herself, and was in the process of raising her 12 Rhode Island red hens. Besides all that, Amelia took care of the daily needs of two goats, one sheep, one guinea pig, and one rabbit. Amelia could drive both the family tractors, and she was a member of the Howard County 4-H Centaurs Horse Club. She ranked #1 in the State (Junior Division) for Horsemanship Contest, #3 in the State (Junior Division) for Oral Reasons in Horse Judging, and she was a member of the Howard County 4-H Horse Bowl Team, which was ranked #1 in the State.

Now, lest you think that Amelia was just about horses and other animals, consider her other interests. She was artsy: She loved quilting, especially with her aunt. She played the piano, beginning at age six. She was good—I heard her practicing one day here in our sanctuary before an upcoming recital that was held in our church building. Amelia studied ballet. She was a member of the youth worship dance ensemble here at the church. They performed during the youth-led Father's Day worship service here at Village just three Sundays ago. She was a member of our children's choir and children's Sunday School. She attended Vacation Bible School every year. Most recently Amelia assisted her mother in leading children's church.

Besides these activities, Amelia had a heart for helping others. She volunteered at PETS, the therapeutic riding farm in Upper Marlboro, helping in any way she could, everything from mucking stalls to grooming horses. She volunteered as a horse wrangler at a local fundraiser for the Make-A-Wish Foundation. She collected old towels and blankets to donate to SPCA. She regularly rescued worms from hot sidewalks and box turtles from unsafe conditions.

Amelia was compassionate and tenderhearted, and not just with animals. One year she came home from the church-sponsored Easter egg hunt, but with no eggs. She told her mother that she could not stand to see the little kids not finding any eggs while the bigger kids got them all. So, Amelia went behind the little guys, taking eggs from her basket and placing them into theirs. Amelia loved to buy or make gifts for people. The only problem was, she could not wait to give the gifts that she had purchased or made. Hence, her mother gladly received many a gift early.

Amelia was a very bright and inquisitive child. She was home-schooled, primarily by her mother, but fully supported as well by her father. In fact, it was Rick who instigated the home-schooling effort, and who supported the family fully financially, and always acted in their best interests. Amelia had a special relationship with both of her parents. Perhaps because she was a later-in-life blessing for both of them, they each cherished their time together with her.

Amelia brought more joy and accomplished more in her 10 and three-quarter years than some people do in a much longer lifetime. I told Barb when we met to discuss this memorial service that in many ways Amelia lived an ideal life. It was not as long as we would have wished, but it was a life filled with happiness and growth and service and fun and loving relationships with family and friends. The true measure of a life is never in length of years. The true measure of a life is in the way that the person touched the lives of others, and with Amelia Grace Dashiell, that measure was very great. The ripples of her life continue to spread far and deep. She was a blessing to everyone who knew her, and we will miss her, more than words can tell.

Rick Dashiell was an original. I had a chance to talk with Rick not too long ago at our annual church picnic on the first Sunday in June. For some reason Barb was not able to be here that day, so Rick and Amelia came together. After the worship service, Rick and I sat together during the picnic meal. Rick was a man of many interests, whose knowledge included world travel, political events, and even theology. In fact, that day we had an extensive discussion about events in the Middle East and how those corresponded with biblical prophesies. We both had traveled in the Middle East, and we enjoyed comparing experiences in Israel and Egypt and other places. I was grateful that I got to spend that time with Rick that day, and I gained some insights into the kind of person he was.

Richard Thomas Dashiell was born March 6, 1947, at Prince George's Hospital in Cheverly, Maryland. He was the youngest of four brothers; his parents were Louis L. Dashiell and Jeanette C. Dashiell. Rick graduated from Northwestern High School in Hyattsville, Maryland in 1965 with an Academic Diploma. It was while attending Northwestern that Rick joined the United States Navy. He served in the Navy during the Vietnam War and was honorably separated after six years. Rick graduated from the University of Maryland with a Bachelor of Science degree. Rick was a project manager for Bechtel Corporation, and he worked for 14 years with the Washington Metropolitan Area Transit Authority as a supervisory construction inspector, helping to construct the Washington, D.C. Metro tunnel system. After that,

Rick was employed with the District of Columbia Water and Sewer Authority, where he served until the time of his death.

Beyond his academic career, and military service, and professional life, Rick was a lifelong adventurer. He loved to travel, with a minimum of baggage and amenities. He visited the Scandinavian countries (Norway, Sweden, Denmark); he traveled throughout the Middle East (Egypt, Syria, Jordan, Israel); and he traveled to many Central and South American countries (including Mexico, Colombia, Ecuador, Peru, Bolivia, Brazil, Chile, Argentina, and the Galapagos Islands).

Rick had a private pilot's license. He trained with a WWII veteran at the Frederick County airport to learn to fly aerobatics. Rick owned a 1943 Stearman biplane, and for years he amazed passengers and folks on the ground with his stunts. Rick once spent several weeks in a dismal swamp in North Carolina. After he crashed a friend's plane in the swamp, being a man of integrity, Rick took it upon himself to repair the plane by hand, while camping out in a tent near the wrecked aircraft. He drew the attention of locals who heard about some pilot living in the swamp, and he was seen around town on his Honda motorcycle with anything from a prop to a wing bungie-corded to the back of his bike. When it came time to test his repairs and the plane was rolled out to the airstrip for take-off, bets were placed on whether Rick would get the rig off the ground. Rick proved them wrong as he roared down the runway and cleared the treetops!

There was another time when Rick was in his late 30s that he and a high school friend (who would later become Amelia's godfather) went into the Everglades in Florida mining for buried treasure (seriously).

His friend Ken had these thoughts to share about Rick:

> I met Rick in 1962. It was in shop class, and we've known each other ever since. (I was making the class project of a very simple bookshelf, and Rick was making a working revolver). We would routinely ask Mr. Gorden, the shop teacher, if he had anything for us to do...and then we'd go into the District of Columbia, and get a bottle of Vertsberger-Hoffbru beer, and drink it on the way back to school. And that was our "wild" days.
>
> Seldom did I ever see Rick take it easy. That just wasn't his style. When I attended our high school graduation, Rick wasn't there. He was already fulfilling his active-duty commitment to the Navy, and I believe he was in the Mediterranean on a destroyer. August of 1965, just before I joined the Army, we went to Teddy Roosevelt's ole hunting camp and had the best time of our lives.
>
> I forget the year Rick moved onto the *Sinbad*, an old rumrunner from the prohibition days. I went to see him, on my way to New York. The guy on

the dock said, "Don't worry; you'll know his boat when you see it. Roofing shingles, and a smoke stack out the top...yep, that's his." After three years on the boat, Rick got antsy again and moved into a VW bus. That provided "flexibility" to see the world. So he spent a summer touring Europe on a motorcycle. That's where he learned to make cheese.

Our treasure project started in 1985. "Spanish Treasure"? In the Everglades? How could he not go? The only treasure we found was the precious time we had together, in a challenging situation, where we each used the skills we learned over the years. I never met a tougher dude. I remember the first time Rick mentioned Barb. "Hey, I'm thinking of getting married... but she's a little headstrong. What do you think?" "If she can put up with you, then go for it." Rick did find treasure after all

... Amelia Grace: We were both in love with her from the start. He couldn't say enough about her. And I never saw anyone more proud. And he was truly impressed with how Barbara managed to keep everything together, and do such a fantastic job with Amelia. He once said, "How did I get so lucky, marrying Barb and then having Amelia?" The answer was simple: Rick was a damn good guy, through thick and thin, always.

As you heard, Rick lived on a boat for years in the Ft. McNair Marina on the Anacostia River. His was the only boat with a smokestack (for his woodstove), and a jacuzzi. Rick traveled across the country on his motorcycle, enjoying many adventures, including heading out during Hurricane Agnes.

Rick was very self-reliant and could fix just about anything. Barb heard more than one person say, "If I were stranded on a desert island, I would want Rick with me." He had a fluid intelligence and a way of solving problems in a completely novel way. One time when his motorcycle chain broke in Montana on a cross-country trip, Rick hiked out into a pasture and cut a piece of barbed wire to fix it so he could get to the next town. The ability to think outside the box let him excel in his work. It was almost as if he had a crystal ball and could see problems and solutions that others could not imagine.

Rick retired in his 30s to travel the world, selling all his possessions (motorcycles, airplane, car). He said he had seen too many folks work their entire lives only to retire and die! He wanted a chance to see the world while he was still able, and he did.

The greatest adventure of Rick's life, he readily admitted, was marrying Barb at age 49 and becoming father to Amelia at 51. But just before Amelia was born, Rick had yet another adventure in him, leaving Barb at home five months pregnant, while he and his old high school chum (Ken again) hiked the Grand Canyon. But after Amelia came along, she and her mother were definitely the focus of Rick's life. Rick was a thoroughly committed father, fully invested in Amelia and everything she did. Rick often told Barb when she tried to buck him for being overly indulgent, "Ah Mom, she's out only one, and she'll be gone before you know it." Of course, Barb is glad now that he was such a doting dad. Rick had various nicknames for Amelia. I heard him refer to her as "Gracie." He also called her "pork-roll," because she was so plump as a baby...Amelia loved that. Rick even allowed Amelia to sleep in the middle between her parents, over Barb's initial protests.

Rick knew that Amelia Grace, Gracie, was a gift from God, and he did not take that gift for granted. I remember the day that Barb presented herself for membership in our church, coming upon her profession of faith and believer's baptism. Rick told me that he wanted to be baptized too, even though he had been baptized previously. Rick explained his decision by telling me, "We do things together as a family." The day that Rick and Barb were baptized, Tracy Colburn, who at the time was a lieutenant colonel in the United States Air Force, was the assisting deacon on Rick's side. Tracy and Rick struck up an immediate friendship based on their military service and their experiences as aviators. Rick was baptized on the basis of his faith in Jesus, as was Barb on that day, and I know that Amelia too had accepted Jesus as her Savior and Lord, and that she lived a faithful Christian life.

So, we don't worry about Rick or Amelia, for we know that they are safe and secure with their Father in heaven. We know that through their faith in Jesus they have entered eternal life with God, and the bliss of heaven that is beyond all the joys of earth. No, we don't worry about Rick, and we don't worry about Amelia, for they are together with God the Father, and with our Risen Lord, and with all the host of heaven.

The pain we feel is not for them, but only for ourselves and those they left behind. There is a hole in our hearts that cannot be filled. Yet, we are not without hope. For we know that God is with us, even in this, and that God will give us the strength and the courage and the faith we need to walk through this vale of tears. Rick and Amelia now have entered the other side of life and begun the greatest adventure of all.

Yes, Amelia has been following me; in my mind, in my heart, she's been following me; Rick too. Barb, I know that Rick and Amelia will be following you and following the rest of those who knew them and loved them. Even more, I know that the love and grace of God will be by your side as well.

In the 23rd Psalm the shepherd king David wrote: "Surely goodness and mercy shall follow me all the days of my life, and I shall dwell in the house of the Lord forever." That is our hope, that is our faith, that is our promise: that goodness and mercy shall follow us all the days of our lives, and that we shall dwell in the house of the Lord forever.

Reflections

The eulogy for Rick and Amelia Dashiell was one of the most difficult I have ever given. The family was hurting, our church family was hurting, and I was hurting. Sudden loss is always difficult, but it is even more difficult when a child and her father are the ones we are mourning.

Because their loss impacted so many people, I needed to express our grief both at the memorial service and during worship on the Sunday after they died. Thus, this chapter contains both the eulogy and the Sunday sermon. The sermon attempted to place this senseless loss in a theological context. The eulogy sought to give voice to our grief, to tell the story of Rick and Amelia, and to lift up our Christian hope.

Eulogists are not immune from grief. I still grieve the sudden loss of Rick and Amelia. In a sense, Amelia is still following me. Her mother, Barb, remained a part of our church family for several years after Rick and Amelia died. Barb was elected a deacon in 2012. Eventually she moved to be closer to her mother, and she was able to begin a new career in another part of the state. But some of her friends in the church have remained in contact with her. And she gave me permission to include the eulogy for her husband and daughter in this book. God gives strength to carry on.

Every Christmas the youth ministry at the church conducts an offering for animals in memory of Amelia. The offering is called "Amelia's Critters." There is a large box in the foyer where donors can place towels, blankets, and pet toys that will be taken to a local animal shelter. Amelia's picture is on the outside of the donation box. It's a way to remember, and pay tribute, and continue the work that she began.

Chapter 6
The Prime of Life

Peter was in the prime of life when I first met him. He was 47 years old, enjoying a very successful career as an electronics instructor, and engaged to be married. He and his fiancée, Belinda, were looking for a place to have their wedding. They were living not far from our church, and they had passed by it many times. They thought it was attractive on the outside, so one day they stopped by to see what it looked like on the inside. I happened to be in my office and met them. We discussed what would be involved for them to be married in our sanctuary, and for me to perform the ceremony. Soon their wedding was on the books, and I was honored to declare them husband and wife on a Saturday in June of 2006.

After getting married in our church, they began attending worship on Sunday mornings. Soon Belinda joined the adult choir that sang for the 11:00 a.m. service. Peter preferred the early service, which began at 8:30 a.m. and was more informal. So, I would see them most Sundays, but often not at the same time. That was okay because I could tell that Peter and Belinda were getting along well.

When Peter first got sick, he did not tell many people about it. Peter was so modest, so unpretentious, that he did not want people to worry about him. Only after his illness got worse did I find out what was going on. In the printed program for the celebration of his life, his wife and her sister wrote:

> When Peter became ill in 2009, it was a very difficult decision for him to give up teaching. He was ill for five years. During that time he was very optimistic and positive throughout his illness, and never complained. He did not allow his disability to interfere with his passion for servicing computers. Even though it took him twice as long, with many frustrations, he never gave up until the job was completed. He was very serious, and well-organized about many things. However, he had a great sense of humor, and was such a natural that oftentimes he did not even realize he was being funny. He had many friends, and remained in contact with them for over 30 years.

Peter had just turned 56 when he died. He left behind his wife of 8 years, his mother, two daughters, and a host of family members and friends.

Eulogy for Peter Franklyn
November 8, 2014

Peter Anthony Franklyn was born on October 26, 1958, in Jamaica. At the age of 3 months, he went to live with his grandparents, who would raise him until the age of 16. Peter's grandfather, and then his grandmother, served as principals of the local elementary school. [You can read about Peter's childhood in the printed program.] Even though Peter moved to England at the age of 16, he always considered Jamaica to be home. There was a girl in Peter's school named Belinda, and they knew each other, but because she was a year older than he, they did not become friends until later in life.

As I said, Peter left Jamaica at age 16 to go live with his mother in London and to complete his secondary education. In 1981, at the age of 23, Peter moved to the United States to continue his college studies in electronics. Peter became what you might call "a computer geek." He excelled in electronics to the point where he was hired by his college as an instructor, and he went on to teach computer science with distinction for over 25 years. In addition to teaching about computers, Peter learned to build and repair computers. His greatest professional satisfaction came from helping his students and from servicing computers for friends and customers.

In his personal life, Peter became the father to two daughters, Alishia, and Althea. Although his marriage to his daughters' mother did not last, Peter remained a devoted father to them for the rest of his life. He helped to raise his girls, and he maintained close contact with them after they became adults and were living on their own.

In addition to computers, Peter had other interests. He loved to play dominoes, and he was a member of a domino club. He was a big fan of cricket, a sport not yet so popular here in America. He was able to watch matches on the computer.

Life was not always easy for Peter. After his first marriage ended, Peter was the victim of an attempted robbery during which he was shot. He was wounded, but he survived the attack and eventually recovered. Because the bullet lodged close to his heart, it was never removed. Unfortunately, the would-be robber who shot him was never caught. You might think such a traumatic event would have had a crippling effect on Peter, but he managed to get on with his life. He did that, in part, by forgiving the man who had shot him, and not allowing that tragic misfortune to ruin his outlook or zest for

The Prime of Life

living. That incident says a lot about the type of person Peter was. Like Jesus, Peter could forgive his enemies.

Peter's life took a turn for the better in 1999 when he was invited to the birthday party of a friend in Philadelphia. He was living in Maryland at the time, but he drove up to Philly on a Saturday for the party, and he stayed over on Sunday to fix a friend's computer. At the birthday party, Peter renewed his acquaintance with another guest, a mutual friend of the honoree, named Belinda. This was the same Belinda he had known casually as a child. Peter and Belinda did a lot of catching up during the birthday party, and then Belinda invited Peter for dinner the following evening. Actually, it was Peter who invited Belinda out for dinner, but she was not accustomed to going out for dinner on a Sunday, so she invited Peter over to her place for a home-cooked meal. That chance meeting at the birthday party would be the beginning of a friendship that would eventually lead to marriage.

It was on a vacation trip back to Jamaica in 2000 that they got engaged. They spent a week staying with Peter's grandmother, who Belinda remembered as the very stern principal of her elementary school. During the week Belinda got to see another side of Peter's grandmother, not the stern principal, but the woman who had raised Peter so lovingly in his early years. It was on the veranda of his grandmother's house, in the moonlight, that Peter proposed to Belinda that they get married. Belinda was surprised because she was still in school and had a long way to go before she would be able to move to Maryland. Well, to make a long story short, the engagement lasted six years. Belinda completed her training to become a nurse and fulfilled her obligation to work at the hospital in Pennsylvania while she and Peter maintained their long-distance relationship.

Finally, in 2005 Belinda moved to Maryland and started planning for the wedding. Another chance meeting took place when Belinda and Peter were looking for a venue for their wedding. They visited a couple of other churches but passing by our church they liked the looks of it, and they decided to stop by and check it out. They met me, and soon I and this church were a part of their wedding plans.

When Belinda and Peter were married right here in this sanctuary on Saturday, June 17, 2006, I was honored to officiate. Peter designed and produced the wedding program himself. Such was the beginning of Peter and Belinda's relationship to this church, and the beginning of their friendship with me.

Their wedding in 2006 was the beginning of eight years of marriage that would bring Peter and Belinda much joy. They traveled as often as they could, visiting Peter's mother in Florida and keeping up with his brother in

Alabama. They made multiple trips back to Jamaica to visit with family and friends and just relax. They enjoyed spending time with Alishia and Althea, as well as friends in Philadelphia and other places.

Peter and Belinda became very faithful in attending our worship services and getting involved in other church activities. During the school year Peter preferred to come to the early service. He appreciated the level of informality, and going to church early on Sundays gave him a chance to do other things during the day as well. Some Sundays when Belinda had to work at the hospital, Peter would come by himself. Other Sundays, when Belinda was singing in the choir at the late service, Peter would find his spot on this side near the windows at the early service.

The last time I remember seeing Peter and Belinda together here in church was not on a Sunday but on a Saturday at our annual seafood feast a few months ago. That was right before Peter had to go into the hospital for surgery. He seemed fine but, I learned later, wasn't feeling too well that day at the seafood feast. But we were raising funds for Stop Hunger Now! and Peter wanted to do his part to contribute.

Although we talked several times after that, the next time I saw Peter was in September at Johns Hopkins Hospital after his surgery. He suffered some numbness in one of his feet, and was having difficulty standing and walking, but Peter was determined to go through the physical therapy. As we visited in his hospital room, Peter told me that he knew there was no cure for the cancer, which had first been diagnosed some five years ago in 2009. He had been through rounds of chemotherapy and radiation treatments. The radiation had caused nerve damage which affected the movement in his right hand, but Peter was not one to make a big deal about it. In fact, a lot of people did not know he had cancer; even some of his friends didn't know, until much later in the progression of the disease.

Peter was a proud man, and a strong man, and he didn't want people to feel sorry for him. So, he kept his medical problems pretty much to himself. After several weeks in the hospital in September, Peter was able to come home and continue his physical therapy there. He was determined to do all he could to get better, even though he knew a cure was unlikely. But he deeply appreciated my prayers for him, and the prayers of our church family.

The last time I saw Peter was when he was back in the hospital a couple of weeks ago. It was just a few days before he died. Belinda and his mother and his aunt were there in the room with him, but they stepped out for few minutes so Peter and I could have some time together. I sat by his bed and talked with him and held his hand and prayed with him. Peter wasn't able to speak then, but I could tell by the movement of his eyes that he was aware

The Prime of Life

I was there and understood what I was saying and praying. Basically, I just assured Peter that he was surrounded by people who loved him, and that he was in God's loving care.

Driving home from the hospital that day, I got stuck in a colossal traffic jam on Route 3 caused by a tractor-trailer that had jackknifed at Waugh Chapel. As I sat in traffic for over an hour, I thought about Peter and reflected on the kind of man that he was. He was a smart man, but he was never arrogant about his intelligence. Peter had an unpretentious and down-to-earth manner about him that made him easy to like. That's probably why so many people counted him as their friend. Peter was a man of integrity and character; you could trust him. Peter was a strong man, but he had a quiet manner about him, and a gentle spirit.

I shed a few tears that afternoon sitting in the car stuck in traffic, because I knew that might have been the last time I would see him on this side of heaven. I'm a pastor, and I believe in God, and I believe in eternal life, but that does not make me immune from the pain of loss. It hurts to lose someone you love. And for his family and close friends, the loss is even more painful. But we are not without hope.

Peter Franklyn lived a good life, and ever the teacher, there are lessons he would want us to learn, even in his passing. He would want us to value the time that is ours, and to cherish the relationships and friendships that make life worthwhile. He would want us to live each day to the fullest, and to waste no time with bitterness or regret. He would want us to continue learning, continue making a difference in the lives of those around us...for that is surely what Peter did.

Of course, his passing is painful for all of us who knew him. Of course, there is sorrow in the hearts of those he has left behind. But even though he is no longer with us in body, he is with us in spirit. And that is our Christian hope. Peter has left his earthly body and received a new and perfect spiritual body from God. Peter Franklyn was a devoted husband, a loving son, a caring father, a faithful friend, and his going leaves a hole in our hearts. But we are comforted by many memories, and by the hope of heaven. Now, may God grant us the grace to carry on, in the sure and certain hope of the resurrection from the dead.

Reflections

After Peter died, Belinda remained in the home they had shared and remained active in our church. But after a while, it was just too lonely for her to be surrounded by so many reminders of Peter, so Belinda made the decision to move to Florida to be closer to her sister. That might have been the end of our relationship, but Belinda stayed in touch with her friends in the church and with me.

Belinda knew that my wife Linda and I, along with our friend, Kathleen, made an annual trip to Florida in the wintertime to play golf and see friends. The year she moved, after learning when we would be in the area, Belinda invited us to come to her house for dinner. That became an annual tradition on our winter trips to Florida. Sometimes her sister would join us for dinner. Other times she invited friends from her new church. Those dinners in her home were times to catch up and renew our friendship. We did not always talk about Peter, but sometimes we did. Belinda had some photos from their wedding mounted on the walls of the hallway leading to her living room. It was obvious that she missed Peter, but she was finding a way to go on without him. Moving to Florida and starting a new job helped. Getting involved in a new church and meeting new friends helped. Staying in touch with friends from her former church helped. Most of all, Belinda was helped by her continuing faith in God and by many memories of her time with Peter. Somehow, she found a way to carry on.

When someone we love dies in the prime of life, it is difficult to move on, but it can be done. Belinda was supported by her family, her friends, and her faith. We still miss Peter, but we are grateful to have known him.

Chapter 7
Complicated Grief

All grief is complicated. There is no straightforward way to mourn the loss of someone you love. Yet, some grief is even more complicated by the circumstances of the loss. Losing a baby is complicated grief. Losing a husband and a daughter in an automobile accident is complicated grief. Losing a husband and father who died in the prime of life is complicated grief. Over the years I have delivered eulogies for persons who died in tragic ways. I tell about some of them in my *Spelunking Scripture* series of Bible study books, including:

- An FBI agent was murdered while working on cold cases at the Washington, D.C. police headquarters. I tell his story in Chapter 1 of *Spelunking Scripture: Christmas*.
- A father with three young daughters was robbed and murdered outside an ATM.
- An 18-year-old was killed in a one-vehicle crash when the pickup in which he was a passenger went off the road and hit several trees and a utility pole. The 19-year-old driver survived. Police believe alcohol was a factor.
- A 42-year-old man died of an incurable disease.
- A father died at age 52, leaving behind six children, two of them in school.
- A boy died at age 16 from cancer. I tell his story in Chapter 3 of *Spelunking Scripture: The Letters of Paul*.
- A 42-year-old mother of two young daughters died after a brief hospitalization.

I gave eulogies for each of those persons who died under tragic circumstances.

In Chapter 4 of *Spelunking Scripture: Acts and the General Epistles of the New Testament*, I tell about my friend Ron Knode, whose death shocked and grieved everyone who knew him. This is what I wrote in that book:

> Ron Knode died on May 31, 2012, at the age of 66. His passing was a tremendous shock and loss to all who knew him. He was so active, so vital, so full of life. It was hard for us to go on without him, especially at the early worship service where he led the music, and in the choir, and in so many other aspects of our church's life. His family and his friends miss him more than we can say. But as much as we miss Ron Knode, we are grateful for the kind of person he was. Ron lived out his faith throughout his life. His roommate at the [Naval] Academy said this about Ron: "He was the only one I knew that could have a good time drinking a root beer in the Steerage under the rotunda. I admired him deep down, because he was dedicated to his religion and lived by its principles." Another classmate said, "Beyond being the smartest and the sharpest guy in our ranks, he was of unrelenting good humor and true to his principles throughout his life."

Now, even a decade after Ron's passing, his friends still have a hard time coming to grips with the fact that he is gone. Our grief is complicated because Ron was so full of life and we did not see his death coming. He died after he suffered a stroke, was briefly hospitalized, and suffered a brain hemorrhage in the hospital.

Eulogy for Ron Knode
Joy in the Journey
June 5, 2012

Ronald Barry Knode was born on January 19, 1946, in Washington, D.C. to the late Daniel P. Knode Jr. and Virginia Knode. He grew up in the District along with his brothers Daniel, Stephen, and Wayne.

Ron graduated from Anacostia Senior High School in Washington, D.C. in 1964. He received an appointment to the United States Naval Academy in Annapolis, Maryland, from which he graduated in 1968. While at the academy Ron competed on the track and field and cross-country teams all four years. Ron loved the Naval Academy; he was a proud graduate. He continued to support the track and field program, even serving as an announcer for track meets.

While serving in the United States Navy, Ron completed his master's degree in mathematics from the Naval Post Graduate School in Monterey,

California. During his seven years in the Navy, Ron was stationed in Japan and later at the National Security Agency at Fort Meade, Maryland.

After his military service Ron began his career in the private sector, working for a series of major defense contractors in the Washington metro area. Ron's final position was Director of Global Security Solutions for CSC. In addition, he was an adjunct professor in the Applied Information Technology graduate program at Towson University.

Ron married his high school sweetheart Judith Herriman in 1968, immediately upon his graduation from the Naval Academy. Ron graduated on June 5 and they were married on June 7. Ron actually met Judy when they were in kindergarten and her family lived just down the street from his. They started dating their junior year in high school. It was a classic case of opposites attracting: Ron was typically vocal and outgoing; Judy was generally more quiet and shy. But their personalities complemented one another, and a loving partnership was formed that grew stronger over the years.

Ron and Judy moved to Bowie in 1974, when he was still working at Fort Meade, to a house on Peach Walker Drive. In 1977 they moved into their home on Pennington Lane, and soon they welcomed three sons into their family, first twins Ross and Todd, then son James. The family moved to Davidsonville in 1985; and after the boys were out on their own, Ron and Judy moved to Crofton.

Ron was a very active and involved father with his three sons, monitoring their homework and encouraging them in their athletic activities—soccer games, sailing, whatever they did. It may have seemed like he was hard on them at the time, with his high expectations and "tough love" approach to parenting, but now they appreciate the strong foundation he gave them.

When his two granddaughters came along, Ron became a doting grandfather. He would do anything for his grandchildren, except let them win at games. He couldn't quite suppress his competitive spirit, so even if he was playing Candy Land or Old Maid with his granddaughter Ellie, she had to *earn* the victory if she was going to beat him.

Ron and Judy had a special relationship. Their time apart served to strengthen their commitment to one another and to inspire them to cherish the time they had together. Judy gave Ron a photo for their anniversary with this inscription:

MISSING!
When you're not around I always feel that something is missing.
Even though I'm strong enough to be alone,
my life just seems more full when you're part of it.

Ron and Judy were devoted to one another, and Judy was by his side to the very end of his life.

We've already heard about Ron's professional career, and his musical gifts, and his love of tennis and his tennis friends. Ron recently joined another tennis group, more of a league, and they have decided to wear black wrist bands in his memory for the rest of the season.

I was Ron's pastor for over 27 years, actually longer than that since he was on the Pastor Search Committee that recommended me to the church back in 1984. Ron was one of our most dedicated church members, and I was privileged to know him as a personal friend.

I did a little research into Ron's history with our church, dating back over 35 years. There was a church Halloween party in 1977 in the church house where Ron served as the auctioneer. Ron was first elected a deacon at Village in 1979, and he was elected three more times: in 1983, 1987, and most recently in 2007, along with Judy. For a number of years Ron served as a high school Sunday School teacher at the church.

After we moved back into our rebuilt church building in 2002, Ron was Carlynn's right-hand man in leading the music at the early service. In 2008 Ron served as our interim adult choir director, doing double duty at both morning worship services. Five or six years ago Ron started leading our Christmas carol sing. He was born to do that! His over-the-top antics leading "The Twelve Days of Christmas" had me laughing so hard I was crying, year after year. Yesterday one of our members, Dr. Caldwell Gaffney, told me that Ron was instrumental in recruiting him for the choir and making him feel so welcome. Ron even had a nickname for him: he called him "Dr. C.J." The last time Dr. Gaffney sang a solo, Ron transposed the music for him into a better key.

Of course, Ron sang more solos in our church than anyone else. He sang for weddings, for funerals, for worship services, for adult choir cantatas, for talent shows, for just the joy of singing. Above all, Ron sang for the Lord. I told our congregation on Sunday morning that Ron was one of the most joyous people I have ever known. Linda reminded me of one song by Michael Card that Ron sang as a solo, "Joy in the Journey." We printed the words on the back of the program, because that could be the theme song for Ron's life.

> There is a joy in the journey
> There's a light we can love on the way
> There is a wonder and wildness to life
> And freedom for those who obey
> And all those who seek it shall find it

Complicated Grief

A pardon for all who believe
Hope for the hopeless and sight for the blind

To all who've been born in the Spirit
And who share incarnation with Him
Who belong to eternity stranded in time
And weary of struggling with sin
Forget not the hope that's before you
And never stop counting the cost
Remember the hopelessness when you were lost

There is a joy in the journey
There's a light we can love on the way
There is a wonder and wildness to life
And freedom for those who obey
And freedom for those who obey.

Twelve days ago, when Ron was taken to the hospital, all of us were in shock. He was such an active, vital, vibrant person that it seemed inconceivable he could be so ill. When Linda and I arrived at Anne Arundel Medical Center that Thursday afternoon, Ron and Judy had already had a very tough day. Ron was nodding off, but he acknowledged our presence and we assured Judy we would do whatever we could to help.

Over the next few days as we visited Ron at Anne Arundel, and then at the Laurel Hospital, we were encouraged by his progress, but most of all we were encouraged by his positive spirit. Even though he had lost the use of his left arm and his left leg, he was determined to get back on his feet. We noticed a tennis ball that he was using to strengthen his grip in his right hand, and to try to get his left hand moving. Judy told me that Maury Sweetin was going to bring him a tennis racket to facilitate his strengthening and rehabilitation.

Last Monday night I got an idea along the same lines. I'd been encouraging Ron in his budding interest in golf. Honestly, I wasn't sure if he would ever be able to play tennis again, but I truly believed he could play golf, even if he had only one good arm and one good leg. Golf has been used to help our wounded warriors returning from the battlefields of Iraq and Afghanistan to recover, even if they had lost arms or legs. I could envision Ron swinging a golf club as a part of his rehabilitation.

I wasn't sure it was a good idea to take a golf club to the hospital, at least not yet, but the week before I had received a broken golf club in the mail. The club was a six iron, and it had been damaged in transit. The grip was still attached to the shaft, but it was wobbling back and forth and of absolutely no use when it came to trying to hit a golf ball. It would have cost more to re-shaft the six iron than it was worth, so I was about ready to throw it away until I thought of Ron.

I separated the grip from the broken shaft and took it to him in the hospital last Tuesday afternoon. He took the grip in his right hand and then shoved it into the curled fingers of his left hand. It was like he was imagining holding a golf club and getting ready to swing it. We had an extended visit that last afternoon together. Ron had Judy and me almost in tears as we laughed at the tales of his golfing misadventures. He never lost his sense of humor.

So, some good was able to come out of that broken golf club. Some good was able to come out of the brokenness of Ron's body. The hemorrhage that Ron suffered in his brain the next morning was so massive that he could not recover. But Ron had indicated his desire to be an organ donor, and because he had taken such good care of himself, some of his organs could be used to help others. Last Thursday afternoon Ron's liver was transplanted into a 60-year-old male, his right kidney was transplanted into a 64-year-old female, and his left kidney was transplanted into a 39-year-old female. Three people were given a new lease on life because of Ron. Of course, Ron Knode was always giving of himself, so it was no surprise that would be his final legacy. Like his Lord and Savior Jesus Christ, Ron Knode gave all he had to give so that others might live. Well done, good and faithful servant: enter your Master's joy!

Now, we are the ones who feel broken. We feel such hurt in our hearts that we wonder how we can carry on. Can any good come out of this for us? YES! We are better people for having known Ron Knode. The memory of his life will live on in us, and by faith, God will heal our broken hearts.

One more thing... Not only did Ron lose the ability to move his left arm and his left leg after the stroke, he also lost his ability to sing. The same area of the brain that controls the left side of the body also controls singing. Ron said that when the speech therapist sang a simple melody and asked him to repeat it, he couldn't for the life of him carry a tune. Well, he's singing now! One more tenor voice has been added to the celestial chorus; his joyous spirit has joined the heavenly host. If heaven could be any better, well, now it is!

Reflections

The death of Ron Knode caused complicated grief because most of his friends and family could not believe he was gone. Ron was one of the most alive persons I have ever known. His illness came on so suddenly, and he died so unexpectedly, that most of those who knew him had a hard time accepting his death. And he left such a hole in our church family.

Ron was a deacon, a Sunday School teacher, a song leader for the early service, a choir member, and a soloist. Ron was the deacon who called me with the news that Rick and Amelia Dashiell had been killed in an auto accident. In so many ways, he was a crucial leader in our church.

But the role he was "born for" was leading the annual Christmas carol sing. As the carol sing approached the December after Ron died, I wondered if we could have it. Frankly, my heart was not in it. I could not imagine having the carol sing without Ron. But people would have been disappointed if we did not have it, so we recruited our choir director, Doug, to lead the event that year.

Doug was a member of the United States Marine Band, and wouldn't you know it, the band had a gig that afternoon that lasted into the evening. So, Doug's wife, Susan, took his place leading the carol sing. Susan was the church's children's choir director, so we knew she could lead music. But we did not know that Susan had been born to lead the carol sing, just as Ron had been born to do it. Susan led the carol sing with such joy that we recruited her to lead it every year after that. We never forgot about Ron, but God showed us we could go on without him.

In a sense, every eulogy is an attempt to discover how we can go on without the person who has died. The eulogy does not diminish how important that person was to our lives. If anything, the eulogy accentuates the importance of that person. But the eulogy also offers hope that our lives can go on, even after great loss.

Chapter 8
Personal Grief

Is it possible for a eulogist to give the eulogy for a family member? Yes. I have done it five times. The first time was after my grandmother died in 1984. We were in Louisville, Kentucky, where I was attending a Doctor of Ministry seminar at The Southern Baptist Theological Seminary. My family was with me since my wife Linda was from Louisville, and she and the kids could visit her family while I was in class.

We got a call from my parents that my mother's mother had died at age 89. Her death was a surprise, but not a shock. She had been in declining health for years, but she was still mentally alert, and we would visit her every time we went to Texas to visit my parents. Now, Mimi was gone.

Instead of driving from Louisville back to Maryland, we drove to Fort Worth. I was okay until I walked into my parents' home and saw my mother. I went into the hallway half bath and closed the door and burst out in tears. After composing myself, I rejoined the rest of the family and we began to plan Mimi's funeral.

Even though Mimi had been a member of Broadway Baptist Church for almost 50 years and knew all the ministers, there was no question that I would give the eulogy for her funeral. I was extremely close to her, having been named after her husband, my grandfather Bruce Shulkey. He died when I was seven years old, and I grew even closer to my grandmother after that. I gave her eulogy during the service in the Broadway sanctuary, and there were no tears, at least on my part. I wanted to do her justice, and I pray I did.

My sister-in-law Ruth (Ruthie) Ford died near the end of 1999. Ruthie had been in declining health for many years. Shortly after Linda and I started dating in 1976, Linda told me that her brother's wife had been diagnosed with a neurological disease that affected her muscles and energy level. Gradually, Ruthie's vision became impaired because the muscles keeping her eyelids open began to fail. Eventually she could no longer drive, and she spent most of her days at home. Yet, Ruthie maintained an incredibly resilient attitude. Whenever we would visit, she never complained about her condition.

Her husband, Skip, took early retirement in 1996, in large part to care for Ruthie. After Skip called to tell us that Ruthie had died, Linda flew to Louisville to be with her brother. I drove to Louisville with our daughter Amy and our son Marc. On the way we passed through Washington, D.C., along the National Mall and by the Washington Monument and the Lincoln Memorial.

Ruthie's funeral was held at her longtime church, St. Matthews Baptist in Louisville, officiated by the St. Matthews pastor. But I gave her eulogy on behalf of the family. And in the eulogy, I compared Ruthie with the monuments we had passed on our way through the nation's capital. At first, it seemed like an unlikely comparison, since Ruthie was small and frail, not tall and mighty. But her spirit was tall and mighty. She inspired all of us.

The next eulogy I gave for a family member was after my father died in 2005. He had been sick with a terminal illness, diagnosed about six weeks before his death. We were there with him and my mother when the doctor gave the diagnosis. My father asked the doctor if surgery were an option. The doctor said, "no," surgery would not cure the disease. My father was crestfallen. He said he would rather die on the operating table than go through the dying process.

After we got back to my parents' house, we met with a hospice representative. My father was too discouraged to participate in the meeting. He excused himself and went to lie down in their bedroom. The hospice representative explained what services they could provide and what we might expect, given how advanced was the illness. After getting hospice set up to come to their house to provide care, Linda and I went back to Maryland.

A few weeks later we returned, shortly before Thanksgiving. To our surprise, my father was sitting up on the couch when we arrived. Apparently our coming back had bolstered his spirits, but his revival would be short-lived.

The next evening I answered the door, and a strapping young man was standing on the front porch with a stethoscope around his neck. He was a hospice nurse who had come to take care of my father that night. In conversation we learned that he had not always been a hospice nurse. He had begun his working life as a roughneck in the oil fields of west Texas. But somewhere along the way he had felt a call to nursing, and he went back to school for training. After graduating from nursing school, he felt called to hospice work, caring for the dying. We were grateful he was there.

After Thanksgiving, Linda and I returned to Maryland. We called my mother every day to check on her and my father, but there was nothing more we could do. About a week later we were eating at a Mexican restaurant in Annapolis when my mother called my cell phone. My father had died. I broke down, even though we knew it was coming. I could not finish eating my enchiladas, so we asked the server to box up our food for us to take home. When we got back home, I sat on the floor of our family room and cried. Linda consoled me, but the tears flowed.

We made plans to return to Texas for my father's memorial service. According to his wishes, his body had been cremated, and his remains would be buried in a cemetery in California, next to the remains of his grandmother, his parents, his stepmother, and his niece (and also his brother, who would die before we could all gather at the cemetery). Once again, I gave the eulogy at Broadway Baptist Church for the memorial service. My brother played a tribute on the piano, and once again, there were no tears on my part. I had a job to do, and I did it as best I could.

About eight months later we gathered at the Cayucos Cemetery in California to lay to rest the remains of my father and his brother. Our immediate family was there, along with aunts and cousins. Once again, I officiated. I read the 23rd Psalm and a poem by John White Chadwick. Then I invited family members to share special memories of my uncle Jim and my father Ted. Then I offered a brief overview of each man's life. After some words of committal and a final prayer, we reconvened at a local country club for a meal together.

My sister died unexpectedly in 2019 at the age of 73. She had been dealing with multiple sclerosis for many years, but it did not seem to be life-threatening. Linda and I had spoken with her recently on the phone, and she seemed to be holding her own. Then, only a couple of days later, she developed pneumonia and was admitted to the hospital. She died after a few days. Her underlying condition may have been a factor. Needless to say, my mother, my sister's two daughters, and the rest of our family were heartbroken.

The memorial service was held in San Antonio, Texas, where she and her husband lived. My sister and her husband did not have a church home in San Antonio, but friends of the family offered us the use of their church. Linda and I drove with my mother from Fort Worth to San Antonio, where I officiated at the service for my sister. My sister's grandson sang a solo, and my brother played a couple of pieces on the piano. I gave the eulogy.

My brother-in-law, Lawrence Miles Ford Jr., died in 2020. We called him Skip, and he was an important part of our lives. He was Linda's big brother, and he called her Sissy. We went to Louisville in the spring of 2019 to help Skip celebrate his 80th birthday, and we returned in December of 2019 to visit again with Skip and his (second) wife Diane.

Although we did not know what was going on at the time, during our visit in December, something did not seem quite right with Skip. Yet, we had plans to meet Skip and Diane in the spring of 2020 in Fort Worth to be with my mother and our daughter Amy, who was planning to come from China where she had been teaching English. Then the COVID-19 pandemic shut down everything.

Amy was able to get out of China and come to Maryland, but our trip to Texas was cancelled. It turned out we could not have met Skip and Diane in Texas because Skip was diagnosed with an inoperable brain tumor about a month after the pandemic began. Skip's friend and former primary care physician went with Skip and Diane to the oncologist to discuss treatment options. Since no treatment would lead to a cure, the friend concurred with their decision to forgo treatment and let the disease run its course. They would engage a local hospice organization to keep Skip comfortable and allow him to remain at home.

Skip was not ready for us to come, so we called him several times every week. He could no longer read or use the computer, but he could talk on the telephone. Finally, in August of 2020, Skip told Linda he was ready for her to come. Since Diane was sleeping in their guest room, Linda took a blowup mattress to sleep in Skip's office. She drove to Louisville, taking the necessary precautions to limit the risk of exposure to the COVID virus.

Linda arrived on Thursday afternoon, and Skip died Friday night. He knew she was there. Months before his passing, Skip had asked me to give the eulogy for his memorial service. Because it still was not safe to have an in-person service, we had the memorial service online. Two friends from Skip's church made the arrangements.

On the way back from Louisville, Linda had decided that she wanted to say something at Skip's service. She gave her tribute just before I gave the eulogy. I had not cried after I heard Skip was gone, but I did have a dream about him. I included that dream in the eulogy.

My experiences in giving eulogies for family members say it can be done. It would not have been unseemly if I had broken down during the eulogies, but I did not want to be a distraction. So, I did my crying and mourning ahead of time. That way I could focus the eulogies on those being remembered, and not on myself.

I have gotten a little choked up from time to time, as I have given eulogies for people I loved. That is okay. People understand. But I have endeavored to keep my emotions in the background so that the eulogy is about the deceased, not about the eulogist. Below is the eulogy I gave for Skip:

Eulogy for Skip Ford
September 5, 2020

Thank you for joining us. I'm Bruce Salmon. Skip was my brother-in-law. I was honored that he asked me to give the eulogy for his memorial service.

Eulogy comes from the Greek, meaning "good word." And I have a "good word" to say about Skip Ford. But first, I have a "good word" from Holy Scripture.

> Have you not known? Have you not heard? The LORD is the everlasting God, the Creator of the ends of the earth. He does not faint or grow weary; his understanding is unsearchable. He gives power to the faint, and strengthens the powerless. Even youths will faint and be weary, and the young will fall exhausted; but those who wait for the LORD shall renew their strength, they shall mount up with wings like eagles, they shall run and not be weary, they shall walk and not faint. (Isa. 40:28-31)

> Do not let your hearts be troubled. Believe in God, believe also in me. In my Father's house there are many dwelling places. If it were not so, would I have told you that I go to prepare a place for you? And if I go and prepare a place for you, I will come again and will take you to myself, so that where I am, there you may be also. (John 14:1-3)

> Listen, I will tell you a mystery! We will not all die, but we will all be changed, in a moment, in the twinkling of an eye, at the last trumpet. For the trumpet will sound, and the dead will be raised imperishable, and we will be changed. For this perishable body must put on imperishability, and this mortal body must put on immortality. When this perishable body puts on imperishability, and this mortal body puts on immortality, then the saying that is written will be fulfilled: "Death has been swallowed up in victory. Where, O death, is your victory? Where, O death, is your sting?" The sting of death is sin, and the power of sin is the law. But thanks be to God, who gives us the victory through our Lord Jesus Christ. (1 Cor. 15:51-57)

> So we do not lose heart. Even though our outer nature is wasting away, our inner nature is being renewed day by day. For this slight momentary affliction is preparing us for an eternal weight of glory beyond all measure, because we look not at what can be seen but at what cannot be seen; for what can be seen is temporary, but what cannot be seen is eternal. (2 Cor. 4:16-18)

> If we live, we live to the Lord; and if we die, we die to the Lord; so then, whether we live, or whether we die, we are the Lord's. (Rom. 14:8)

This is the Word of the Lord. Thanks be to God!

I have another "good word" to share, from the beautiful obituary written by Skip's wife, Diane, and by Skip's sister, my wife Linda.

> Lawrence Miles Ford Jr. (Skip) died peacefully at home on August 21, 2020. He was born on April 1, 1939 in Louisville, where he lived his entire life. He was preceded in death by his parents, Lawrence Miles Ford Sr. and Dorothy Helen Langley Ford, and his childhood sweetheart, Ruth Ann 'Ruthie' Brumley, to whom he was married for 40 years.
>
> Skip was a proud graduate of Campbellsville University, Class of 1958, and the University of Louisville, with a B.A. in 1961. Skip's first career was teaching in the Bullitt County School System. He next began a 44-year career with Loevenhart's Clothing Store. At the age of 67, he entered a CPE unit for chaplaincy training, followed by service as a volunteer chaplain at the University of Louisville Hospital, and as an ombudsman.
>
> After his wife Ruthie died in 1999, Skip met and married another great love, Diane. They were blessed with 14 years of love and happiness.
>
> Skip's life was marked by deep and meaningful relationships. He was a member of St. Matthew's Baptist Church for 40 years, serving in many roles including deacon chair, young adult teacher, devotional writer, and a loyal friend to all. He participated in a spiritual formation group for 25 years, along with five sacred companions who studied together weekly. Skip lived out his calling to ministry through personal giving. His life was filled by forming relationships with countless people in the ministry of caregiver. He could always be counted on to give wise advice and spiritual encouragement. He was a true friend to many.
>
> He is survived by his loving wife, Diane; his stepdaughters Jennifer Gibbs (Tim) and Amy Swindle (Patrick) and their daughters Alexandria and Cassandra Swindle; his sister, Linda Salmon (Bruce); his nephew, Marc Salmon (Stacey Grumet); his great-niece Ford Salmon; and his niece Amy Salmon. Skip loved his family, his friends, his professions, his church, and above all his Lord. Thanks be to God!

As I was reading the obituary that Diane and Linda wrote, I was struck by the number "40" or "40-something." Skip was married to his first wife, Ruthie, for 40 years. Skip was a member of St. Matthews Baptist Church for 40 years. Skip worked at Loevenhart's Clothing Store for 44 years. I knew Skip for 44 years. Skip was "Uncle Skippy" to our daughter Amy for 46 years, and he was "Uncle Skip" to our son Marc for 40 years. He was friends with some of you for 40 years, or more.

There was a lot of stability in Skip Ford. When he got into something, he stayed with it. He was in the Renovaré Group for 25 years. He was married to Diane for 14 years. There were so many qualities about Skip that I admired—his deep and growing faith, his genuine love and concern for his family and his friends, his sense of humor, his good heart. If Skip was your friend, he was your friend for the long haul.

Earlier in his life, Skip wrestled with the possibility of being called into the ministry. Church was always important to him, and for a time he considered whether God was calling him into full-time Christian service. Well, ultimately, Skip decided that he was not called to be a pastor; but he had a ministry, nonetheless. He had a ministry as a schoolteacher. Then he had a ministry in his 44 years at Loevenhart's. In his work in the clothing store, Skip did far more than make people look good. He made people feel good. Skip was a people-person.

Ken Grossman, whose parents owned Loevenhart's, and who worked with Skip in the store, wrote this tribute:

> Last Friday I lost a best friend, mentor, and surrogate uncle when Skip Ford passed away. I have known Skip virtually my whole life, as he started working at Loevenhart's, my family's business, even before I was born in 1957. Skip's father, Larry Ford Sr., managed the Loevenhart's leased Florsheim shoe department. Combined between Skip and his dad, they had over 80 years invested in our family business. The Fords were as much Loevenhart family as any of us.
>
> When I started working at the store in 1982, Skip was the store manager and sportswear & furnishings buyer. He also became my boss because, as my father put it, I could not have a better teacher. Skip was smart, trustworthy, and had a keen eye for style and fashion. He was meticulous in everything he did. He was a valued partner for my dad, Lee Loevenhart Grossman.
>
> It took a village to accomplish what we did over the many years at Loevenhart's, and Skip was a pillar of strength through it all. Key steps along the way that Skip championed were the move from 3rd & Market Street downtown to Oxmoor Center in 1971, the renovations in 1985, and the closing of our store in 1995. We could not have done it without Skip. Between Skip and his protégé Barbara Dye, our store had incredible interior displays, show windows, and presence. As Skip liked to say, our displays and windows were our "silent salesperson."
>
> Skip's devotion to St. Matthews Baptist Church and his church family were integral to both his success and the success of our store. Some of our best employees were members of St. Matthews Baptist including Alice Willingham, Anne Thrasher, Barbara Dorton, and Hilda Berryman, just to name a few. Skip was affectionally known and always called "Mr. Ford." It was both a title and a sign of the respect he commanded in his leadership. He had deep relationships with so many of our employees. Skip lived by the

golden rule in the way he treated customers, employees, and friends. He taught us to always do the right thing.

In a unique way the store was guided by a mix of Jewish and Christian theology, with a Jewish owner supported by many of the Baptist faith. The third partner in the leadership triumvirate of my father's generation at Loevenhart's was the Reverend Bob Kilgore, who was also introduced to my father by Skip. Mr. Kilgore was retired from Crescent Hill Baptist Church. Another source of part-time employees were divinity students from The Southern Baptist Theological Seminary. The store set high standards for outstanding customer service, integrity, and family values.

Skip gave me needed support and guidance. He taught me to become a store buyer, manager, and life lessons too numerous to mention. We enjoyed attending trade shows together in New York, Chicago, and Las Vegas. And yes, Skip played the slot machines and always won! There were quite a few good times. Skip and I took many bike rides together. On holidays when the store was closed, we played doubles tennis with my dad and brother Phil in what we called "Grossman Cup" tennis, the long-standing prize being an old Styrofoam cup.

My favorite Skip story is when Skip finally agreed to have a cocktail with me at the Plaza hotel in New York City. It was a beautiful night overlooking 5th Avenue in Manhattan. When Skip's drink arrived, sirens shrieked, and a fire truck went screaming by. With Skip's quick wit he says, "I guess they are announcing I'm here. They didn't have to send the fire trucks for my first drink." His sense of humor I will miss.

I have so much respect and love for Skip. My life and so many others would not be the same without him. Skip's lessons, love, and friendship will endure forever.

Skip also had a ministry taking care of his mother and taking care of Ruthie as her health declined over the last 25 years of their life together. He had a ministry as a volunteer hospital chaplain and a nursing home ombudsman.

Skip had a ministry as a Sunday School teacher and a deacon and a Renovaré leader and a leader of the neighborhood Bible study group that he started. One of Skip's former pastors at St. Matthews, Altus Newell, wrote this about Skip:

When I became Skip and Ruthie's pastor in the '70s, what impressed me most was Skip's gentle, patient, loving care of his wife. Ruthie's physical disabilities made it difficult for her to walk and to accomplish other physical tasks. Skip was always there at her side to help her— patiently, gently, lovingly—exemplifying true fruit of the Holy Spirit. When the church asked him to become a deacon, I visited with them to talk about it. It was apparent how Skip and Ruthie saw this not as a position to be achieved, but as a ministry to be considered carefully and prayerfully, and to be entered unreservedly. The outcome of that decision has blessed St. Matthews significantly ever since.

Skip was not a pastor, but he had many ministries throughout his life. He served God and he served other people every step of the way.

In 2019 Skip celebrated his 80th birthday. Skip was born on April 1st, and he wanted to have some fun with it. He threw himself a party that would have been fun for an 8-year-old. There were balloons, and balloons, and more balloons.

Skip and Diane invited some friends to come to their house for the celebration. Linda and I were in charge of the food, but Skip and Diane took care of the cake, because not just any birthday cake would do.

After the meal we gathered in a circle the family room to talk about our experiences with Skip. I wrote a song, and halfway sang it in his honor, "The Ballad of Skip Ford," based on the theme song from the *Beverly Hillbillies* TV show. David Garrard performed some magic tricks. None of us could figure out how David did it, even though we were only six feet away from him. Skip ended the festivities with heart-felt appreciation for his friends.

None of us imagined then that Skip would have only one more birthday. But that birthday party was like a snapshot of Skip's life. He enjoyed it, and he was grateful. Skip did not take his blessings for granted. I'm not going to sing the song I wrote about Skip, but here it is:

The Ballad of Skip Ford*
By Bruce Salmon

Come and listen to my story 'bout a man named Skip,
For 80 years he's been taking quite a trip,
Until today when he stops to celebrate
With his wife and his sister and his friends and a cake.
(Lawrence Ford Jr.? No way—Skip!)

Now Skip was born back in 1939 –
A long time ago, but like a vintage wine
He just keeps gettin' better as the years roll along,
And so, we sing his praises in this ditty of a song.

It was no joke—Skip was born on April 1,
Although he's always ready for some teasing and some fun;

He can be sentimental, and serious too,
But mainly he's just there for me and for you.

Now Skip was born to Dorothy and Larry Ford,
And from the beginning he was cherished and adored,
But then came little sissy to join the family
And Skip made room for Sissy in the Ford company.

Besides his folks and Linda, Skip found another love –
Her name was Ruthie, she was given from above;
Skip had no other sweetheart—she was the only one.
And so they were married at 20 and 21.

Then for a little while, Skip taught school,
His heart was in it, but he knew he'd be a fool
If he turned down the offer to work at Loevenhart's,
So, he joined his daddy; they were buddies from the start.

Now Skip was a churchman, for a while at Ninth & O,
But as his faith grew stronger, he found another place to go;
It was Saint Matthews Baptist where Skip really grew
Into a deacon and a teacher and a leader through and through.

Skip also grew at Loevenhart's with his good friend Lee,
Who gave him more duties and responsibility,
Until he made vice president, in charge of purchasing
All manner of men's clothing, making Skip's heart sing.

Now Skip had some troubles, as all people do,
First, he lost his dad, then Ruthie got sick too.
Then Loevenhart's closed in 1995;
But Skip found a reason to continue to thrive.

Skip was devoted, watching Ruthie and his mom;
It wasn't easy, but his faith kept him strong;
Skip watched over Ruthie until the very end,
As he'd watched o'er his mom, time and again.

His heart was broken, but Skip carried on
Until the second love of his life came along;
Her name is Diane—Skip really loves her too,
They're almost perfect together, like paper and glue.

Personal Grief

Today is April 1st, but Skip is no fool—
He knows he is blessed; he lives the Golden Rule:
He treats all others as he would want to be,
And they love him back, like a big family.

Well, now it's time to say "goodbye" to Skip and all his friends;
He would like to thank you folks for kindly dropping in.
You're all invited back again to this locality
When Skip hits 85 or 90, or even 103!
(*with apologies to Flatt and Scruggs' "Ballad of Jed Clampett")

Well, Skip did not hit 85 or 90 or even 103. He died at 81, but they were 81 good years! It's not that life was always easy for Skip. It was not. There were times of crisis and challenge.

Skip was extremely close to his father. They worked together at Loevenhart's. They were more than father and son; they were best friends. But on October 17, 1968, his father, who appeared to be in good health, suffered a massive heart attack and died in Skip's arms. His father was only 61.

Another crisis came about five years later. Skip's sister Linda had married and had a baby. Life was good. But in 1973 Linda's husband Doug was diagnosed with acute leukemia. Nine months later Doug died at age 32, leaving Linda and their young daughter, Amy, to face life alone. Skip was there for Linda and Amy, just as he was there for his mom when his father died.

Then another crisis came in 1976. Skip's wife Ruthie was diagnosed with an incurable chronic illness that led to fatigue, failing vision, and deterioration of the muscular system. Skip and Ruthie would deal with her illness for the rest of their marriage, along with caring for his mother until she died in 1996. Ruthie died at the end of 1999. Skip was devastated, but he found the faith to carry on.

Another crisis came when Skip was diagnosed with Parkinson's disease. Skip had always been so active, playing tennis, riding his bicycle; he even took up golf. After Ruthie died, Skip went with us one year on a winter golf trip. But with the onset of Parkinson's, Skip had to give up tennis and golf and riding his bicycle.

Yet, the last 14 years of Skip's life were extremely happy. That's because he found a new love—Diane. Diane was the missing piece of the puzzle for Skip. Skip loved Diane, and Diane loved Skip. They loved each other to the very end.

A few months ago, Skip was diagnosed with an incurable brain tumor. He was offered two options: medical treatment which might prolong his life, but with serious side effects, or hospice care to let the illness run its course. Skip and Diane chose the second option. Skip said he was going to ride the bicycle until the wheels fell off, and when that happened, they could put the bicycle back in the garage, and we know where that is.

Well, Skip kept riding the bicycle until the wheels fell off. He spent these last two months connecting with his family and his friends and telling them he loved them. It gave us a chance to tell Skip we loved him too.

The night Skip died I had a dream. I don't remember ever dreaming about Skip before, but he was in my dream that night. In the dream, Skip was going to look for a new place to live, and I was with him. We were in different vehicles, but we pulled up in front of a house that had four cars in the driveway. We got out of our vehicles and walked toward the house, and I wondered if this was the house Skip wanted to look at. The four cars in the driveway made me think this couldn't be the place. Then I looked next door. There was another house, high up on a hill. I said to Skip, "That must be the place. But we can't walk all the way up there. It's too high up." Then the dream ended.

Now, generally I don't put much stock in dreams. Most of my dreams are crazy, and that one was a little crazy. But as I thought about it, maybe there was some truth to it. I remembered what Jesus said: "In my Father's house there are many dwelling places. If it were not so, would I have told you that I go to prepare a place for you? And if I go and prepare a place for you, I will come again and will take you to myself, so that where I am, there you may be also" (John 14:2-3).

In my dream, Skip was looking for a new place to live. And there was the house, high on the hill, with many dwelling places. We could not walk all the way up there. It was too high up. But Jesus came, and took Skip to himself, so that where Jesus is, Skip may be also. Skip is home. He's finally home.

Skip Ford was a man of faith. If he could say anything to us today, I believe he would tell us to have faith too. There is a song that was released some years ago by the Christian music group 4Him. Skip, almost, could have written it. The song puts it like this:

> I believe in faithfulness
> I believe in giving of myself for someone else
> I believe in peace and love
> I believe in honesty and trust
> but it's not enough
> For all that I believe may never change the way it is
> Unless I believe Jesus lives

Where there is faith
There is a voice calling, keep walking
You're not alone in this world
Where there is faith
There is a peace like a child sleeping
Hope everlasting in He who is able to
Bear every burden, to heal every hurt in [your] heart
It is a wonderful, powerful place
Where there is faith

There's a man across the sea
Never heard the sound of freedom ring
Only in his dreams
There's a lady dressed in black
In a motorcade of Cadillacs
Daddy's not coming back
Our hearts begin to fall
And our stability grows weak
But Jesus meets our needs
if we only believe

Where there is faith
There is a voice calling, keep walking
You're not alone in this world
Where there is faith
There is a peace like a child sleeping
Hope everlasting in He who is able to
Bear every burden, to heal every hurt in [your] heart
It is a wonderful, powerful place...
Where there is faith
(Billy Simon, Copyright 1989, River Oaks Music Co., Nashville, TN)

Reflections

Delivering the eulogy for a family member requires the eulogist to deal with his or her emotions beforehand. I experienced outbursts of tears after my grandmother died and after my father died. After my sister-in-law died, there was a 12-hour car trip that allowed plenty of time for reflection. After my sister died, I discussed the upcoming memorial service with my dermatologist while in her office for my bi-annual checkup. The doctor offered a critique that helped me to handle a mix of emotions. After my brother-in-law died, there was a dream that I incorporated into the eulogy.

We do not react to every death in the same way, but reacting in some way is an important step in the grieving process. Writing the eulogy can be a step in the grieving process. So is delivering the eulogy. Grief is felt and expressed in many ways.

Delivering the eulogy for a family member is a choice, not an expectation. My friend, Dr. James Langley (who is the subject of Chapter 10), asked me to give the eulogy for his wife. Dr. Langley was an ordained minister, a former pastor and denominational executive, an outstanding preacher, and a mentor and role model for many ministers. No doubt he could have given a superlative eulogy for his wife, but he asked me to deliver her eulogy so that he could focus on supporting the rest of his family.

After my mother-in-law died, I did not give her eulogy. That was because she had been close to her pastor who gave the eulogy, and because my energies were devoted to supporting my wife and our children.

When I have given the eulogy for family members, it was because they had asked me to, or because I was in the best position to tell their stories and to help our family move through our loss.

Chapter 9
Well Done

How do you measure a life? What criteria do you use? Professional accomplishments? Academic achievements? Financial success? Family relationships? Service to others? In a sense, the eulogy is a reckoning, an accounting, a measuring of a person's life. The eulogist makes decisions about what is important to tell about the person being remembered. And in the end, there is a summation, a conclusion, an assessment of what it all means. That is why the eulogist must be barefoot: she or he is standing on holy ground.

In a column in *The Washington Post* (March 9, 2021), Steven Petrow wrote that after his parents died, he and his siblings wrestled with what to have inscribed on their grave markers. They agreed to put "Journalist and Professor" on the marker for their father, and "Beloved by all" on the marker for their mother. Petrow said that his father's identity was defined by his professional achievements, his "résumé virtues." His mother, who had long managed a psychotherapy practice, work that she was proud of, nevertheless was more focused on how she would be remembered at her funeral, what Petrow calls "eulogy virtues." On Facebook, Petrow asked his friends how they wanted to be remembered. Most responded with a chorus of eulogy virtues such as "kind," "loyal," "compassionate," "she raised great kids," and "someone who tried to make the world a little better." Only two of his friends wanted to be remembered for their professional accomplishments.

The eulogy seeks to relate what the deceased person did (résumé virtues) with who the person was (eulogy virtues). We are more than our accomplishments; we are persons in relationships with other persons. And the quality of our relationships is an indication of who we are. One of my favorite verses in the Bible is Micah 6:8: "He has told you, O mortal, what is good; and what does the Lord require of you but to do justice, and to love kindness, and to walk humbly with your God?" That verse encapsulates a combination of résumé virtues and eulogy verses, both what we do and who we are.

The goal for most of us is to live a good life. Again, how we define a "good life" is a matter of interpretation. Ancient philosophers such as Socrates,

Plato, and Aristotle identified such virtues as prudence, temperance, fortitude, and justice. Paul in his first letter to the Corinthians identified the Christian virtues of faith, hope, and love. And, as Paul said, "the greatest of these is love" (1 Cor. 13:13). Jesus talked a lot about the primacy of love. As it says in 1 John 4:12, "if we love one another, God lives in us, and his love is perfected in us." Perhaps that is how we should measure a life: the degree to which God's love is perfected in us.

Over the years I have conducted funerals for many godly people who sought to live a life of love. Below is the eulogy for one such person. Mae Fenrick was a member of our church who exemplified the Christian virtues of faith, hope, and love. Her greatest ambition was to allow God's love to be perfected in her.

Eulogy for Zenobia Mae Fenrick
April 12, 2014

Zenobia Mae Murden was born on June 5, 1935 in Cleveland, Ohio. Zenobia Mae was the second of six children born to Henry and Annie Murden.

At a young age Zenobia Mae moved with her family to Annapolis, where she attended private kindergarten at the Helen Jones Pre-School at College Creek Terrace. She began her education at a young age, and she would continue to be involved in education for the rest of her life. Zenobia Mae attended Stanton and St. Mary's Elementary Schools and she graduated in 1954 from the historic Wiley H. Bates High School.

During her childhood and adolescent years, Zenobia Mae was involved in many extracurricular activities. She loved music, she played sax in her school band, and she sang in school and church choirs. Zenobia Mae learned to be of service at an early age. She was a backyard preschool teacher, she delivered groceries for the sick and homebound, and after she graduated from high school, she volunteered to be a nanny to the children of a family friend. Indeed, her entire life would be marked by her service to others.

Zenobia Mae enrolled in Bowie State Teachers' College (now Bowie State University) where she graduated with a Bachelor of Science degree and later with a master's degree in education. I joked with Mae that she and I were both Bowie State graduates, except my master's from Bowie State came much later than hers.

Z Mae began her teaching career in Anne Arundel County as a primary classroom teacher. As a classroom teacher, and later as a guidance counselor, Mae loved working with children at all levels. In both Anne Arundel County and in Prince George's County, she served as a guidance counselor for at-risk children and for children with special needs. She also taught in Warren County, North Carolina, and was Dean of Housing and Student Affairs at St. Paul's College in Lawrenceville, Virginia. While accompanying her late husband on military assignment, she served as a librarian in Heidelberg, Germany. Her teaching career was long and varied. She taught in the Aeosop Math Program at Adams Park in Annapolis. She was a Pupil Personal Worker at Tall Oaks Vocational High School here in Bowie. She was a guidance counselor at Oak Hill Juvenile Detention Center in Ft. Meade, Maryland. She served as director of the Spruilll Summer Enrichment Program for children and youth. She was an adjunct professor at Sojourner Douglas College. And she served as interim director of the Anne Arundel County Head Start Program. You can see that two of the greatest investments of her life were education and helping young people to learn and develop and grow.

Besides her family, the greatest investment of her life was her faith in the Lord Jesus Christ. She was baptized at a young age at First Baptist Church, Annapolis. She attended Bible study and Sunday School at First Baptist Church in Annapolis, and later here at Village Baptist Church. In fact, Mae was a member of my Sunday School class, and she also attended the ladies Tuesday morning Bible study here at the church. For many years she attended the Baltimore National Baptist Convention. She served as chairperson of Christian Board of Education Committee at First Baptist, Annapolis. She taught Sunday School and Vacation Bible School. She sang in the children's and adult choirs. She started the children's church program at First Baptist. She was a 70-year member of First Baptist Church in Annapolis. When Mae and her family began to attend our church a few years ago, she continued to attend First Baptist as often as she could. Gradually, over time, the convenience of our church being basically across the street from her house won out, and she joined the Village Baptist Church congregation, with mixed emotions. She grew to love our church and to be an active part of it, but she never relinquished her ties to her original church home, First Baptist Church of Annapolis. That was okay with me. I could understand her devotion.

Mae obviously loved the Lord, and she served the Lord all her life by serving God's people. When Mae wasn't involved with her teaching career or her church activities, she found other ways to be of service. She was always ready to lend a helping hand to those in need. She was a volunteer at the Crownsville State Hospital, and even sang in a choral group for the patients there. She also was involved with many worthwhile service groups and civic organizations, such as the Phi Delta Kappa and Alpha Kappa Alpha sororities, the Delicados Inc., the Retired Teachers Association, and the Eastern Star. I joked with her daughters that Mae must have attended a lot of meetings! But that's who she was—she loved people. She especially loved being involved in the development of people, young and old.

Mae was absolutely devoted to her family and friends. She was a loving mother and grandmother and great-grandmother, a caring sister, and sister-in-law, and aunt and great-aunt. One of the great joys in her life was traveling with family and friends. She embraced life to the fullest. She had an ability to look for the good in everyone. We will remember her for her patience, her kind words, her sense of duty and purpose, her love of children, and her dedication to the Lord.

The last year or so of Mae's life was difficult for her and her family. She spent more time in hospitals, nursing homes, and rehab facilities than she spent at home. During 2013 I would guess that I visited with her at least once a week, because she was being treated at so many different places. I was sorry that she and I spent so much time together in those circumstances, but I was grateful that I got the chance to know her more fully during those many visits.

Of course, I already knew her before that long series of hospitalizations and recuperations. She was a dedicated member of our church, regular in worship, and as I said, faithful in attending my Pastor's Sunday School class. But she was, by and large, a quiet person in those settings, never one to toot her own horn or to brag about her many accomplishments. Occasionally she would make a comment during Sunday School, or during the Tuesday morning ladies Bible study here at the church, but she was never one to want to be the center of attention. She was a humble person, in the best sense of the word.

But during those many visits we had together over the last year or so, we had a lot of meaningful conversations, and I came to understand more of who she really was, and I came to appreciate the depth of her compassion for others, and the depth of her strong Christian faith. I came to see that beneath her calm and composed exterior, there was a calm and composed heart. That sparkle in her eye was a sign of a sparkle in her spirit.

Mae spent most of 2014 at home, and I had a chance to visit with her on a number of occasions there. Her daughters Denise and Debbie were very attentive to her, making sure that she was comfortable and well cared-for. Home was where Mae wanted to be, and home is where she lived out the last days of her life on earth. Now, she has gone from her home on earth to her home in heaven. As Paul said in his letter to Timothy, she fought the good fight, she kept the faith, she finished the race. She has received the crown of the righteousness which the Lord, the righteous judge, has awarded her for a life of faith and devotion and love and service. She has heard her Savior say, "Well done, good and faithful servant, enter your Master's joy!"

Of course, there is sorrow in the hearts of those she has left behind. Mae was a devoted mother and grandmother and great-grandmother, a loving sister, a caring aunt and great-aunt, a faithful friend, and her going leaves a hole in the hearts of those she has left behind. But her family and friends are comforted by many memories, and by the promise that she has received her heavenly reward. Mae is at rest and at peace with her Father in heaven. Now, may God grant peace to all those whom she loved, and those who loved her; peace and the grace to carry on, in the sure and certain hope of the resurrection from the dead, first by our Lord and Savior Jesus Christ, and to all who have placed their faith in him.

Reflections

I have never given a eulogy for a perfect person, but I have given eulogies for many persons who lived exemplary Christian lives. In those instances, the eulogy truly is a "celebration of life." It's not that those persons never made any mistakes or were without flaws. Even the best persons among us are imperfect. We are saved by God's grace, not by our own righteousness. As Paul wrote in Romans 3:23-24, "since all have sinned and fall short of the glory of God, they are now justified by his grace as a gift, through the redemption that is in Christ Jesus."

All have sinned, yet redemption is a gift of grace. The light of Christ can shine brightly in the lives of those who have been saved by faith and who have been devoted to following him. They are not perfect, but they have been redeemed, and it shows by the way they live.

In delivering eulogies, I sometimes quote from the updated version of James Montgomery's hymn, "Servant of God, well done."

> Servant of God, well done!
> Rest from your loved employ;
> The battle fought, the victory won,
> Enter your Master's joy.
> ....
> The pains of death are past,
> Labor and sorrow cease;
> And life's long warfare closed at last,
> Your soul is found in peace.

We can say "well done" to those servants of God who have entered their Master's joy. We can celebrate their faithfulness and their examples of Christian living. It is not ours to judge, but it is ours to give thanks for lives well-lived.

Chapter 10
The Rest of the Story

James Langley served for more than 20 years as the executive director of the D.C. Baptist Convention. I first met Dr. Langley in 1977 after I was called to Montgomery Hills Baptist Church in Silver Spring, Maryland, as associate pastor. It was my first full-time ministry position after seminary, and I was looking for role models to help me learn how to be a minister. My primary role model was Rev. Donnell Harris, the pastor at Montgomery Hills, but as I got to know Dr. Langley, he became a role model too.

In 1984, without telling me, Dr. Langley gave my name to the Pastor Search Committee at Village Baptist Church in Bowie, Maryland. I was not looking to leave Montgomery Hills, but Dr. Langley thought I was ready to move from being an associate pastor to being a pastor. So, he gave my name and phone number to Leslie Parreco, who was on the Village Pastor Search Committee. Leslie called me at my home, identified herself, and said that Dr. Langley had given them my name. She wanted to know if I would be interested in meeting with her committee.

This was a call out of the blue. I was not expecting it and not prepared for it. I knew little about Village except that it was a sister church in the D.C. Baptist Convention. It probably was because Leslie had told me that Dr. Langley had given them my name that I agreed to meet with her committee. If Dr. Langley thought we might be a good fit, then I should check it out.

Well, Village did call me to become their next pastor in the fall of 1984, and I began my service there on January 1, 1985. I served at Village as pastor for 33 years until I retired in 2018. And during all that time my friendship with Dr. Langley continued and grew.

We became golf buddies. Eventually we formed a group of Baptist ministers who played golf together most Thursdays, including Dr. Langley's successor at the D.C. Baptist Convention, Jere Allen. I have a picture of Dr. Langley and Dr. Allen and some other members of our Thursday group that was taken at my house at our annual Christmas get-together. We are all wearing matching shirts in the picture and standing in front of some golf balls mounted in cases and hanging on the walls of our family room.

My friendship with Dr. Langley was not limited to the D.C. Baptist Convention or our Thursday golf group. My wife Linda and I used to meet Dr. Langley and his wife Jean for lunch at the National Gallery of Art in Washington, D.C. Jean worked for the National Gallery and later volunteered as a docent. Whenever there was a new exhibit, they would invite us to tour the exhibit and then join them for lunch. One evening I invited the Langleys to meet us at the Goddard Space Flight Center in Greenbelt, Maryland for a lecture, and then to have dinner together at a Chinese restaurant in the shopping center across from Goddard.

Jean died unexpectedly in 2002. She was on her way to work at the National Gallery when she suffered a medical emergency and later died. We were all heartbroken. To my surprise, Dr. Langley asked me to give the eulogy at her funeral, held at the Briggs Memorial Baptist Church in Washington, D.C. I was surprised because Dr. Langley could have asked any number of pastors to give her eulogy. But he trusted me to tell her story, and I was honored to do so. Linda and I continued to meet Dr. Langley for lunch at the National Gallery of Art after Jean died, and we got together on other occasions. Simply put, Dr. Jim Langley was one of my best friends.

After I retired in 2018, Linda and I had to figure out where we would go to church. The first Sunday after I retired, we went to First Baptist Church of the City of Washington, D.C., where Jim Langley was a member. We sat with him that Sunday, and we continued to sit with him in church every Sunday after that. The last Sunday in May of 2018 we were in Texas visiting my mother. When we returned, I got a message from Jim's daughter Carol that he was in the hospital. We rushed downtown to be with him. Jim's son, Jim Jr., was there, along with Carol and their sister Marilyn. Jim was unresponsive, but I believe he knew we were there. He died a few days after that.

I led the committal service at the cemetery the following Saturday. Then a month later I gave the eulogy at the memorial service at First Baptist Church of the City of Washington, D.C. Most people at the service knew Dr. Langley well. So, much of what I might say about him they already knew. But I knew a side of Jim Langley that many of them might not have known. And so, I could tell the rest of the story. When my book, *Preaching for the Long Haul: A Case Study on Long-Term Pastoral Ministry* was published in 2019, the dedication page read:

In Loving Memory of
James A. Langley
(1925–2018)
Pastor, Preacher, Poet, Mentor, Friend

Eulogy for Jim Langley
July 28, 2018

I first met Jim Langley back in 1977. I had been called to the Montgomery Hills Baptist Church in Silver Spring as associate pastor, and Dr. Langley was the executive director of the D.C. Baptist Convention. As a young minister fresh out of seminary, I was looking for mentors and role models. My primary mentor was Rev. Don Harris, the pastor of Montgomery Hills. But the more I got to know Dr. Langley, the more he became a mentor and a role model too.

In 1984 Dr. Langley recommended me to the Pastor Search Committee of the Village Baptist Church in Bowie, Maryland. Had it not been for his recommendation, the search committee never would have contacted me. I was not looking to leave Montgomery Hills. I did not have my résumé "out there." But Dr. Langley saw potential in me, and without telling me, he gave my name to the search committee. The church called me, and I became pastor of Village Baptist Church on January 1, 1985.

Dr. Langley retired from the D.C. Baptist Convention as executive director in 1991, and Dr. Jere Allen came as the new executive director in 1992. Shortly after that, I was attending a pastors' meeting in which both Dr. Langley and Dr. Allen were present. Knowing I was a golfer, they asked me if I would be interested in playing a round of golf with the two of them. Would I? I readily accepted. We played at the Rock Creek Golf Course, just up 16th Street here in Washington, D.C. It was the beginning of a golf friendship that would continue to this day. Eventually that golf friendship became a Thursday golf group, comprised of Baptist minister friends.

After Jim stopped playing golf with our Thursday group, he would often call me on Fridays to see how the round had gone. His standard question was, "Did anyone make a hole-in-one?" I relayed that to the group, and it became a kind of mantra from then on. If anyone by chance hit a tee shot close to the hole on a par 3 the shout rang out: "Call Dr. Langley!" Well, a year and a half ago, I finally made my first hole-in-one (not with our Thursday group, but on a trip to Florida). And the very first person I called was Dr. Langley! I called him from the airport in Tampa, and then I sent a text message to everyone in our Thursday group. The text message simply said: "I called Dr. Langley!" and they all knew what it meant. Jim even wrote a poem about my hole-in-one, which is displayed in our home next to the hole-in-one plaque with the ball and score card. But my friendship with Jim was about far more than golf.

My wife Linda and I used to meet Jim and his wife Jean at the National Gallery of Art, where Jean worked and volunteered. We would view the exhibits and then have lunch together. On another occasion we went to the

Goddard Space Flight Center in Greenbelt, Maryland to hear a lecture from the author of the book, *Galileo's Daughter*, and then to have dinner. Jim was a role model for me, and Jean was a role model for Linda. I admired Jim's intellect, his people skills, his leadership abilities, his preaching ability, his Christian commitment, his humble demeanor, his sense of humor, and so much more. Linda admired Jean for her spunk, her independence, her intellectual curiosity, her love of art and music and beauty, her love of people, and so much more. Jim and Jean were married over 50 years. They were more than husband and wife: they were life partners. On one occasion, after having spent the day with the Langleys, Linda said to me, "That's the way I want us to be after we've been married 50 years." Tragically, Jean died suddenly and unexpectedly in 2002.

But theirs was a true love story. It began while they were both students at Southwestern Baptist Theological Seminary in Fort Worth, Texas. Jim spotted Jean across the room, in the seminary library. How fitting that the two of them, for whom the love of learning was a lifelong mutual passion, should first meet in the library!

Although they were both born in Alabama, Jean's family had moved to Massachusetts, and then to Alexandria, Virginia, when she was growing up. Jim and Jean would not meet until they were seminary students in Fort Worth. Jim, who had served our country during the Second World War, felt called to the ministry, and followed his brother Ralph to Baylor, where they both were involved in the Youth Revival Movement. After that, it was on to Southwestern Seminary in Fort Worth, where Jean was pursuing a Master of Religious Education degree, and that fateful meeting in the seminary library.

Jim and Jean were married in 1951 in the sanctuary of the Fountain Memorial Baptist Church here in Washington, D.C. After Jim received his Bachelor of Divinity degree from Southwestern, he and Jean moved to Princeton, New Jersey, so he could pursue a master's degree there. Following Princeton, they returned to Texas, so Jim could enroll in the Doctor of Theology program at Southwestern.

Jean got a job teaching first grade in the Fort Worth public schools. The first time I met Jean, she told me that she had known my grandfather, Dr. Bruce Shulkey, for whom I was named. My grandfather was the assistant superintendent of public schools in Fort Worth, in charge of all the elementary schools. Back then he personally interviewed and hired all the new elementary school teachers and principals. Jean told me that my grandfather had interviewed her, and he had offered her a job teaching first grade in Fort Worth. So, I had a connection with the Langleys I hadn't known about.

The Rest of the Story

In 1955 Jim and Jean took a two-and-a-half-month trip to Europe, before beginning a new adventure in their life together. In 1957 Dr. James Langley was called to become the pastor of the Pennsylvania Avenue Baptist Church in Washington, D.C. It was after moving to the District that their four children were born: Carol, James Jr., Jane, and Marilyn. As the kids were growing up, Jean was a stay-at-home mom who devoted herself to her children, but who also supported Jim in his ministry at the church.

Let me summarize Jim's ministry by quoting from the District of Columbia Baptist Convention website history page:

> James A. Langley served as executive director from 1970 through 1991.
>
> [Dr. Langley said,] "Racial reconciliation has been one of the major thrusts of my ministry. It is incumbent upon Christians to do all we can to overcome moral problems in the world today,"
>
> [That] was exemplified in his 13 years as pastor of Pennsylvania Avenue Baptist Church, and in his leadership of the D.C. Baptist Convention, where 22 African American congregations were added during his 21-year tenure.
>
> His thought-provoking editorials in the *Capital Baptist* were equal in quality of the best syndicated columnists in *The Washington Post*.
>
> Under his leadership, 32 churches were added, the Convention elected its first woman as president, a ministry was begun to embassy personnel, new work was established for Hispanics and Asians, and there was expansion of all the programs in the Convention.

Such is a brief overview of Dr. Langley's life, but what I really want to talk about is the kind of person Jim Langley was. At the risk of being trite, let me summarize his character by saying that he was a "gentleman and a scholar."

First, he was a gentleman. I'm not just saying he was courteous and polite and considerate and thoughtful of others and well-mannered, which of course, he was. I'm saying he was a gentle man. Let me illustrate with a few stories.

Jim and I were playing golf together at the Bowie Golf Course in suburban Maryland. We stopped at the turn, between the 9th and 10th holes, to get something to eat in the clubhouse. Jim ordered a grilled cheese sandwich, to go. He was intending to eat it on the back nine, so he put the grilled cheese sandwich in the golf cart. We were standing on the 10th tee box, waiting to tee off, when we looked over and saw a big black bird swoop into our golf cart and grab Jim's grilled cheese sandwich. Now, Jim was not one to use colorful language. In fact, not a foul word came out of his mouth (no pun intended). But the look he gave that bird…said it all. We laughed about the purloined grilled cheese sandwich for years after that.

Another time Jim and I were playing golf in Alabama. We were down for his brother Ralph's charity golf tournament. After Ralph retired as pastor of First Baptist Church in Huntsville, the church put on a golf tournament in his honor. We had entered a team in Ralph's tournament. Our team was comprised of Jim Langley, Jere Allen, my son Marc Salmon, and yours truly. When we arrived at the golf course, Ralph Langley came out to greet us in the parking lot. I had bought colorful matching golf shirts for our team, which the four of us were wearing. Ralph made some wisecrack about our golf shirts looking like pajama tops. Now, that was the first time I had ever met Ralph. But it gave me an insight into the dynamic between the two brothers. Ralph was always giving his younger brother Jim the business. Well, Ralph made a disparaging remark about our golf shirts, and Jim didn't say a word. It so happened that our team was right behind Ralph's team on the golf course during the tournament. We came to a par 3 over water. We watched as Ralph hit his tee shot into the pond. Again, Jim didn't say a word. But I could see a hint of a smile come over his face. After Ralph's group finished the hole, our group teed off. Jim proceeded to hit his tee shot over the pond and onto the green. Once again, Jim didn't say a word, but I could see more than a hint of a smile on Jim's face. Ralph had baptized his ball, but Jim had hit the green with his tee shot! Jim would have the last word after all.

One more story about Jim, the gentle man: Last fall Jim called and suggested we meet up during the annual meeting of the D.C. Baptist Convention. He said he had something he wanted to give me. Well, we did meet up. In fact, we sat together during the opening plenary session at People's Community Baptist Church off New Hampshire Avenue in suburban Maryland. After the session, we were walking together through the building on our way to the parking lot, so Jim could give me some items he had in the trunk of his car. I'm not kidding, every few feet, people stopped us to say "hello," not to me, but to Dr. Langley. These were people from various churches in the D.C. Baptist Convention who had known Dr. Langley over the years. Now remember, Dr. Langley retired as executive director of the D.C. Baptist Convention back in 1991, a long time ago. But he was still held in such high regard by so many people that they wanted to stop and greet him as we passed by.

Dr. James Langley was a gentle man, a kind man, a deeply good-natured man, a humble man, a godly man. He exemplified the scripture from Philippians which our friend Paul Clark read earlier: "Let the same mind be in you that was in Christ Jesus…" Christ was his example in the way that Jim Langley lived. As Jim wrote in his hymn, "Almighty Father, Full of Grace," "O fill us, Holy Spirit, free: Indwell that we may Christ-like be."

The Rest of the Story

The second attribute I use to describe Jim Langley is that he was a scholar. His poetry is one evidence of that. He used so many literary and historical allusions that some of his poems required footnotes to understand. Jim had a brilliant mind, and he devoted his intellect to helping deepen our understanding of the Christian faith. Jim's poem, "Glimpses of the Great" is like an overview of modern civilization. In the poem he references:

Shakespeare	Martin Luther King Jr.
Pascal	Victor Hugo's Jean Valjean
Tolstoy	Emily Dickinson
Madame Curie	Nobel
Lincoln	Raoul Wallenberg
Anne Sullivan	Malala Yousafzai
Helen Keller	Handel
da Vinci	Beethoven
Wilberforce	Churchill
Vivaldi	Nelson Mandela
Bach	Wilbur and Orville Wright
Niemöller	Marconi
Pasteur	Einstein
Vermeer	Neil Armstrong
Clara Barton	C.S. Lewis

Clearly, Jim was a man who was well-read. He had a deep appreciation for the arts, science, literature, and the struggle for human rights.

Tim and Zena were kind enough to put some of Jim's poems into booklet form, so you could have them to read. Many of Jim's poems were published in the quarterly journal, *Christian Ethics Today.* We are grateful to Pat Anderson, the editor of *Christian Ethics Today,* for publishing many of those poems, and for giving us permission to put them into this booklet. Some of Jim's poems became hymns, such as those we sing today.

Jim Langley was a scholar in another way: he maintained a lifelong love of learning. For several years Jim and I went together to St. Mary's Seminary in Baltimore for the annual Dunning Lecture series. St. Mary's is a Roman Catholic seminary, but they have an ecumenical institute that sponsors a lecture series, inviting renowned scholars to come and give presentations. One year, Jim and I went together to hear Bishop N.T. Wright, one of the foremost New Testament scholars of our time. On our way up to the lecture, we stopped at a diner on the west side of town, just outside the Baltimore Beltway. As we were eating, a couple came over and spoke to Jim. They were former church members, who had known him as their pastor at

Pennsylvania Avenue Baptist Church. Another year we went together to St. Mary's Seminary to hear a lecture by Dr. Bruce Metzger, a distinguished professor at Princeton who was chair of the committee that translated the New Revised Standard Version of the Bible. Jim had known Dr. Metzger when he studied at Princeton. After the lecture, there was a book signing, and Jim had the chance to chat briefly with Dr. Metzger face to face.

Even though Jim was retired, he maintained a love of learning, and a love of teaching others. Kate Campbell told me that right after she joined First Baptist, Dr. Langley invited her to meet with him. They met for 45 minutes, and Kate said Dr. Langley made sure that she understood the importance of church membership. Apparently that lesson took, because Kate became a key leader here at First Baptist. Jim was not just a member here at First Baptist, he helped out wherever he could—whether it was teaching, preaching, counseling, or even serving through Martha's Table. His daughter Carol shared with me a sermon that Jim preached here at First Baptist on a Sunday morning in 2015. In that sermon Dr. Langley discussed theories of the atonement, how the cross of Christ made atonement for our sins. First, Jim explained the Moral Influence theory of the atonement, perhaps best summed up in the devotional classic *The Imitation of Christ* by Thomas à Kempis. Then Jim explained another theory of the atonement, the Substitutionary view, that Christ died in our place. To illustrate, Jim told a story from his own life.

It was during the Second World War, when Jim was serving in France, during the Battle of the Bulge. Jim's unit was providing medical supplies to the U.S. 7th Army. As the casualties mounted, members of Jim's company were selected to move from the rear echelons to the front lines to supplement the combat troops. Jim was told to pack and be ready to go into battle. Needless to say, he was fearful. He had a premonition that in combat he likely would not survive. Two of his classmates had been killed in Normandy, and a cousin had been killed in the Italian campaign. But he was under orders, so he packed his gear and waited. It was then that another American soldier, a Jewish G.I named Kauffman, was substituted in Jim's place. Instead of being sent into combat, Jim was put in charge of medical supplies for a newly formed American Prisoner of War General Hospital to care for thousands of German prisoners. After the war, Jim was anxious to learn how Kauffman had fared. He contacted the Army Records Division and was relieved to learn that Kauffman had survived the war and returned safely to the United States.

In the sermon Jim said that he had often thought about two Jews who took his place. One unwillingly took his place during the Second World War, but that Jew survived. Two thousand years earlier, however, another Jew willingly took his place, and it cost him everything. Jim closed the sermon with lines from his poem, "Atonement: Mystery and Reality."

> It was for me—the bitter tree,
> For all, He suffered in our place...
> Atonement rests [alone] on grace.

After Jim died, I called many of our mutual friends to let them know. One couple I called were Earl and Jane Martin, who served Temple Hills Baptist Church in Maryland before becoming missionaries with the Southern Baptist Foreign Mission Board and then field personnel with the Cooperative Baptist Fellowship. Earl sent this tribute to Jim: "We were life-long friends, beginning as students at Southwestern. He was one valiant servant of the Lord—open-hearted and innovative—a poet and staunch evangel of the Good News." The last time Earl and Jane Martin were in this area, they stayed with us in our home in Bowie. We arranged to meet Jim downtown at the National Gallery of Art and spend the day together. Jim and Earl Martin were kindred spirits—godly men who read the Bible with open minds and open hearts, and who put their faith into practice. Robert Cochran joined us for lunch that day at the Gallery, since Robert knew the Martins from his time in Europe.

How then can we summarize the life of Jim Langley? Jim articulated the theme of his life in his poem, "Bringing Transcendence in Play." I cannot read it like he did, but allow me to say the words, and you can imagine Jim's resonant voice.

> If I can lift up hope to a soul despairing,
> Or strive for justice with the will to stay,
> If I befriend another in burden-bearing,
> Forgive a wrong through Christlike caring,
> Oppose any of the myriad evils with daring,
> Or guide a wanderer lost to find the way,
> Show compassion to the poor from day to day,
> Or inspire defeating fears allay,
> I shall share in bringing transcendence in play.

Jim Langley did share in bringing transcendence in play; we caught a glimpse of God in him. Jim Langley followed Jesus all the days of his life, and now he has joined the host of heaven, and heard his Master say, "Well done, good and faithful servant."

As Peter wrote: "Blessed be the God and Father of our Lord Jesus Christ! By his great mercy he has given us a new birth into a living hope through the resurrection of Jesus Christ from the dead..." (1 Pet. 1:3). Yes, we have a new birth into a living hope.

Perhaps the last poem that Jim wrote was a single stanza titled "I Will Not Fear." The poem was written this year. Somehow, Jim knew his time on earth was drawing to a close. The last Sunday we were together here in church, it was the next-to-last Sunday in May, we had a conversation right over there after the service. For some reason, Jim wanted to make sure that I was still willing to give his eulogy, as I had done for Jean. I told him, "Of course, we agreed on that a long time ago. Don't worry about it."

That week Linda and I made a trip to Texas to see my mother. Jim sent me an email asking me to tip my cap when we passed "Lovers' Lane" near the Colonial Country Club golf course. "Lovers' Lane" (actually, Mockingbird Lane along hole #15) was a place that he and Jean had spent part of their courtship.

After we returned from Texas, Carol sent us word that Jim had suffered a fall and was in the hospital. Linda and I rushed down to Georgetown University Hospital and spent some time with Carol and Jim Jr. and Marilyn at Jim's bedside. We talked to him, and touched him, and told stories about him, and gathered around his bed for prayer. It was difficult to tell whether he was responsive or not, but somehow, I believe he knew we were there. The final poem that Jim wrote was this:

> A radiance shines from eternity,
> In every age and sphere
> From the same power that sets us free,
> Therefore come what will, I will not fear.

Another poet, William Wordsworth, wrote:

> And when the stream
> Which overflowed the soul was passed away,
> A consciousness remained that it had left,
> Deposited upon the silent shore
> Of memory, images and precious thoughts,
> That shall not die, and cannot be destroyed.

Deposited upon the silent shore of our memories are images and precious thoughts of a loving father and a grandfather, a gentle man and a scholar, a faithful minister and a church member, a mentor and a friend, our beloved Jim Langley. He has gone from us in body, but he remains with us in spirit. Thanks be to God.

The Rest of the Story

Reflections

The eulogy for Jim Langley was longer than most eulogies I have given because I wanted to tell the rest of the story. Many people who attended his memorial service at First Baptist Church of the City of Washington, D.C. knew Dr. Langley well. They knew him through the church and through the D.C. Baptist Convention. But I knew a side of Dr. Langley that many of them did not know. And so, I endeavored to do more than provide an overview of his life; I sought to elucidate the kind of man he was.

When Jim's daughter Carol called and asked me to come to the hospital, my wife Linda and I rushed downtown. Carol met us at the Metro station, and she drove us the rest of the way to Georgetown University Hospital. During our visit in Jim's room, standing by his bed, Linda said to his daughters Carol and Marilyn and his son Jim Jr., "He is one of Bruce's best friends." I had never thought of it like that, but it was true. Dr. James Langley had started out as a mentor and role model, but over time Jim Langley became one of my best friends.

It has been my honor to give eulogies for many friends. Jim's daughter, Carol, a physician who took a job with the U.S. government so that she could move back to Washington, D.C. and live with her father, asked us to come to the hospital after he became ill. We maintained contact with Carol after that. When Carol died in 2020 at the age of 62, Jim's son and other daughters asked me to conduct her funeral. The funeral was held at the cemetery since the COVID pandemic made indoor gatherings unsafe. I was honored to give the eulogy for Carol, as I had done for her parents.

When you serve as pastor of the same church for 33 years, you make many friends along the way. And in each eulogy for a person whom I knew well, I sought to provide some insights into that person's character. A eulogy is more than a chronology of a person's life; it is a good word about who that person was. I had a good word to speak about Jim Langley because I knew firsthand who he was.

Chapter 11
Mother of a Friend

Beverly lives across the street from Linda and me. She has a key to our house. Whenever we are going to be traveling, we give Beverly a copy of our itinerary. We stop the newspaper delivery and the mail, but Beverly keeps an eye on things. She is a trusted friend.

I had seen Beverly's mother, but I had never met her. She lived with one of Beverly's sisters, not too far away. Beverly's mother often would come to visit at her daughter's house. Sometimes I would wave as I saw her walking from the driveway to Beverly's front door.

I knew that Beverly was very close to her mother. They saw each other regularly, and sometimes they took trips together. I knew that Beverly's mother was getting up in years, but I did not know that she had been sick. When Beverly told me that her mother had died, I could tell that she had not been expecting it. It was a shock to Beverly, her sister, and the rest of the family. Grief is always difficult, but it can be even more difficult when we do not see it coming.

Beverly asked me to conduct the funeral for her mother. It would be held at a local funeral home, with the burial at a cemetery in another part of the county. I knew both the funeral home and the cemetery well, having conducted many funerals in both places. However, this funeral would be held in the early days of the COVID-19 pandemic before vaccines were widely available. I had not been vaccinated yet, nor had most people. Beverly assured me that the funeral home was taking necessary safety precautions. There would be limited seating in the funeral home chapel and, of course, we would be outside at the cemetery. This would be the third in-person funeral I had officiated during the pandemic. The first two were held entirely outside at cemeteries, with face masks and social distancing. This funeral would be both inside and outside. I was somewhat hesitant about gathering inside with a group of people, but Beverly needed someone to officiate at her mother's funeral, and she asked me to do it.

Normally, when I would conduct a funeral for someone I did not know, I would meet with the family and talk about their loved one and seek to gain an understanding of that person's life. In-person meetings with the family were not advisable at this time, so I asked Beverly to write out an overview of her mother's life. Beverly had already shared with me what kind of person her mother was, but the overview would provide a timeline so that I could tell her mother's story in the eulogy. Beverly and one of her nieces were also going to speak during the funeral, so that provided some assurance that we would say what was most important about her mother.

There was limited seating in the funeral home chapel, with chairs spaced out and people wearing face masks. Instead of a soloist, a violinist provided special music both at the funeral and at the cemetery. Again, we followed safety protocols. Singing during the pandemic was discouraged, since virus droplets could be projected. The violinist did a good job setting the tone for the funeral and providing music as people were gathering around the grave at the cemetery. To accommodate more people, the funeral home had set up cameras in the chapel that would live-stream the service to those who had mobile devices in their cars in the parking lot outside.

After the service at the funeral home, I followed the hearse in my car to the cemetery. Before the pandemic, I would ride with the funeral director in the hearse to the cemetery. But to provide for social distancing, I drove my own car in the funeral procession, with lights flashing to keep us together and to alert other drivers.

After the committal service at the cemetery, I stood to the side as mourners dropped flowers on the casket. A few people came over to speak to me, but there were not the usual handshakes and hugs, except for one fellow who extended his hand and thanked me for the service. Since we were outside and it was cold and I was wearing gloves, I shook his hand and conveyed my condolences. Such was the awkwardness of funerals during the pandemic. Normal gestures of consolation were necessarily inhibited.

The next day Beverly came over to our house to thank me again for conducting the service for her mother. I gave Beverly a printed copy of the eulogy in case she wanted to read it and share it with other family members.

Funeral Service for Agnes M. Cheri
Beall Funeral Home, Route 3, Bowie, Maryland
February 8, 2021, 12:00 p.m.

Musical Prelude   Violin

On behalf of the family, we welcome you to this celebration of life in loving memory of Agnes M. Cheri. We have gathered here today to remember

Agnes, to celebrate her life, and to comfort one another in our loss. With the sure conviction that God is here, let us turn to the Father in prayer.

Our Father in Heaven,

We have gathered in this time of remembrance to rest our hearts beneath the shelter of your loving care. We have gathered to say goodbye to this beloved mother and grandmother and great-grandmother and great-great grandmother, and sister and friend, but also to seek your strength and consolation as we deal with our sorrow and come to grips with our loss. As we mourn, help us to mourn in hope, knowing that you have prepared a place for Agnes, and that you are with us even now. Give us, O God, a new awareness of your presence in our midst, and give us the grace to remember with gratitude, and look to the future with hope. Give comfort to all who mourn, O God, and give us hope in the promise of eternal life. This we pray in the name of Jesus, who rose victorious from the dead, and who lives forevermore, that we might live victorious with you, Amen.

Hear now words of grace and peace that come from Holy Scripture (Psalm 23, New Living Translation)

> The LORD is my shepherd; I have all that I need. He lets me rest in green meadows; he leads me beside peaceful streams. He renews my strength. He guides me along right paths, bringing honor to his name. Even when I walk through the darkest valley, I will not be afraid, for you are close beside me. Your rod and your staff protect and comfort me. You prepare a feast for me in the presence of my enemies. You honor me by anointing my head with oil. My cup overflows with blessings. Surely your goodness and unfailing love will pursue me all the days of my life, and I will live in the house of the LORD forever.

In John 14:1-4 Jesus said: "Do not let your hearts be troubled. Believe in God, believe also in me. In my Father's house there are many dwelling places. If it were not so, would I have told you that I go to prepare a place for you? And if I go and prepare a place for you, I will come again and will take you to myself, so that where I am, there you may be also."

Eulogy for Agnes Cheri

Her parents named her Agnes. She was born on February 13, 1934 to Mollie and Horace Norwood. She had two siblings: Albert and Joan. Agnes was a happy-go-lucky child, and she kept that happy spirit throughout her life.

Agnes would go on to have six children herself, and she worked hard to provide them with unconditional love and support. She made sure that she did not miss any events in her family's lives that were important to them. Agnes loved ALL her family and friends, and she made sure they knew it.

Agnes met Frank (Sam) Cheri later in life. She married Sam (third time's a charm), and she was blessed to be with him for decades before his death in 2004. She was the apple of his eye; he treated her like the queen she was in life. To see them together brought so much joy, as it was clear they had true love. They were so kind to each other, and they were always together, day and night. Even though he was a [Washington] fan, and she was a Dallas Cowboys fan...well, you can imagine. Sam would send her to her room if she started talking trash during the game—of course, she never went to her room.

Agnes joked that she raised two of her grandchildren, as she babysat for them often—Tina and Little Billy. She told the same stories year after year. Agnes (and Sam) took Tina to the toy store when she was little, and Tina could not make up her mind. Agnes would say, "Make it up fast, or you get nothing." So, Tina would grab something fast! Billy (still known as Little Billy to Agnes, even as an adult) would cry at the daycare when she would drop him off, and each time she promised to buy him a Slurpee if he would stop crying. Agnes and Sam loved going to Grandparents Day at Ariel's school, and they were so proud that she knew how to do the "chicken dance" that she and Sam learned there. At pool parties she would do that silly dance again and again.

For years, Agnes and Sam had a produce stand in the D.C. Farmers' Market off Florida Avenue. Agnes would disappear for an hour or so daily. When family members would call her, Sam would say she was "touring," because she had to talk to everyone all the time. Once her daughter Beverly sent a gorilla with balloons to the market for her birthday, and it totally freaked her out, but Sam knew in advance and was cracking up at her response.

Agnes had a passion for gambling that spanned decades. It didn't matter if it was playing cards (where she never wanted to "fold 'em," even if she had a pair of deuces, because she always hoped she would catch the right card). Her favorite card game was 3-card poker. And then there was Bingo—she would have gone every day if she could have. During COVID she had to resort to playing Bingo in the garage at Rod & Reed a few times. Agnes, Sam, and her mother went to Bingo faithfully, even in snowstorms. Going to casinos—Vegas was her favorite place to vacation, and she got to go there with Sam and her mom, then several times with her daughters and her son Dewey. Dewey surprised her when he decided in 2019 to go on the trip to Vegas with

Mother of a Friend

them. Agnes was beside herself with happiness that her son was there. He was a king to her, probably because he was the only boy. She also enjoyed all the vacations with family to so many places, from Ocean City, to Alaska, and every place in between. She loved Nashville because she got to meet Johnny Cash's sister. She was always a huge fan of Johnny Cash.

Agnes was up for any party (and she was the life of the party with the special little dance moves she made up). While she liked dancing with the girls, she liked it more dancing with the men. A few years back she moved in with her daughter Betty, who was her main caregiver. She also had help from many others, especially Beverly and Gene, who would gladly stop by to help with anything she needed (like her special order for Chinese food; and McDonald's fish; and chocolate milkshakes). The family thanks Gene for all the love and help he gave Agnes during the last few years. Agnes liked it when Gene would hold her hand to cross the street. One time Beverly took her hand and she slapped it and said, "GENE will hold my hand!"

Agnes was truly a special individual to every person she ever met, even for just a short time; she called them her friend. She was the most caring person this world has seen. While so many family and friends already miss her more than words can truly express, we all know that she knew how much she was LOVED.

Last Monday was her last day on this earth. Betty was holding her hand when she died. It happened so fast that Beverly did not have a chance to say goodbye. But that's okay. There really wasn't anything they needed to say to each other. Now, God has taken Agnes by the hand, as she has crossed over to the other side. That is our hope.

Agnes has left behind her earthly body and received a new spiritual body from God. Of course, there is sorrow in the hearts of those she has left behind. Agnes was a faithful wife, a loving mother and grandmother, a proud great-grandmother, a caring sister, a trusted friend, and her going leaves a hole in our hearts. But we are comforted by many memories, and by the promise that she has received her heavenly reward.

Now, Tina would like to say a few words. Also, Beverly would like to share about her mom.

Dear Father of the Risen Christ,
With you, there is no death. Our beloved Agnes has gone from us but is at home with you. And so, our Father, we don't worry about Agnes. We know she is in your joyous presence. The journey of her life on earth has ended, and she has entered into eternal life with you. Help us O God, to move through

this time of sadness. Help us not to forget her, but to learn to live without her. Help us to cherish her memory, and to find the faith and strength to carry on.

We pray especially for her daughters and son and grandchildren and great-grandchildren and great-great grandchildren. We pray for her sister and her friends here and far beyond. May the memories of her time among us bring many occasions to smile and to give thanks.

Strengthen us, our Father, as we face some lonely and difficult days ahead. May the pain we feel now yield to sweet remembrances and memories of a love that will never die. We trust in you, our loving Heavenly Father. Hold us close in your everlasting arms. This we pray in Jesus' name, Amen.

Musical Tribute   Violin

Committal Service for Agnes Cheri
Fort Lincoln Cemetery, Bladensburg

We have gathered here in this quiet place of beauty and remembrance to lay to rest Agnes Cheri. Even though there is sadness in this hour, we are not without hope. As the violin plays, let us remember and give thanks.

Musical Tribute   "Walk the Line"   Violin

The apostle Paul wrote in his second letter to the Corinthians: "So we do not lose heart. Even though our outer nature is wasting away, our inner nature is being renewed day by day. For this slight momentary affliction is preparing us for an eternal weight of glory beyond all measure, because we look not at what can be seen but at what cannot be seen; for what can be seen is temporary, but what cannot be seen is eternal" (4:16-18).

In his poem, "Abiding Love," John White Chadwick wrote:

It singeth low in every heart,
We hear it each and all,—
A song of those who answer not,
However we may call;
They throng the silence of the breast,
We see them as of yore,—-
The kind, the brave, the true, the sweet,
Who walk with us no more.

Mother of a Friend

'Tis hard to take the burden up,
When these have laid it down;
They brightened all the joy of life,
They softened every frown;
But oh, 'tis good to think of them,
When we are troubled sore!
Thanks be to God that such have been,
Although they are [here] no more!

More home-like seems the vast unknown,
Since they have entered there;
To follow them were not so hard,
Wherever they may fare;
They cannot be where God is not,
On any sea or shore;
Whate'er betides, Thy love abides,
Our God, for evermore.

In the sure and certain hope of resurrection to eternal life, we commend to Almighty God: Agnes Cheri. We commit her remains to the ground: earth to earth, ashes to ashes, dust to dust. The Lord bless her and keep her, the Lord make his face to shine upon her and be gracious unto her and give her peace. Amen.

"I have fought the good fight, I have kept the faith, I have finished the race" (2 Tim. 4:7). Rest in peace, rest in peace, in God's mercy, rest in peace.

Musical Tribute   "Amazing Grace"   Violin

This concludes the Committal Service for Agnes Cheri. May we go in peace.

Reflections

For months after the funeral, every time I would see Beverly outside in the neighborhood, I would ask her how she was doing. She always confessed that she was still grieving. I assured her that such grief is to be expected, especially since her mother was such a significant part of her life.

Beverly wondered if her "prolonged" grief was unusual. I told her it was not. For many mourners it takes a year, or longer, to get back to "normal." Holidays and birthdays and other special occasions likely would be reminders that her mother was no longer with her physically. But her mother would always be with her in spirit.

According to Jelena Kecmanovic, founding director of the Arlington/DC Behavior Therapy Institute and an adjunct professor of psychology at Georgetown University, the pandemic made grieving more difficult due to religious and cultural mourning rituals being disrupted. In a *Washington Post* article (Nov. 4, 2021), she quotes Holly G. Prigerson, professor of sociology at Weill Cornell Medicine and co-author of *Bereavement: Studies of Grief in Adult Life*: "In the current environment, we are likely to see more people whose grief doesn't lessen with time." In fact, a new disorder has been added to the guide for diagnosing mental health problems, the Diagnostic and Statistical Manual of Mental Disorders (DSM-5-TR). The new disorder has been identified as "prolonged grief disorder" (PGD).

From Professor Kecmanovic I learned that "PGD can be diagnosed no sooner than one year after the death of a loved one." That's because the first year after losing a loved one is filled with reminders—every Thanksgiving, Christmas, birthday, holiday, or other special occasion accentuates the loss. Typically, after the first year, mourners find a way to manage their grief and to reinvest their lives in other pursuits and relationships. But for about 1 in 10 people who have lost a loved one, they struggle with PGD after the first year. According to Professor Kecmanovic, symptoms can include "a daily, intense yearning for the deceased or a preoccupation with thoughts or memories of them." Additional symptoms can include "avoidance of reminders of the loss, intense emotional pain, difficulty engaging with others and with life, emotional numbness, feeling that life is meaningless, and intense loneliness."

I was not able to maintain contact with family members for every person I eulogized, but I could maintain contact with Beverly. Her grief did not dissipate in an instant, but it did lessen over time.

Funerals during the pandemic were difficult. The usual rituals were disrupted, and consolation was more difficult to convey. But God was with us, and healing did come.

Chapter 12
Benediction

The benediction is a "good word" at the end of a funeral or memorial service or worship service. It comes from the Latin, meaning "good speech," or to "speak well." It affirms our Christian hope and sends us forward with God's blessing. Sometimes the end of a life is a benediction. That is how I felt after my friend Maury Sweetin died.

He had been sick for many months with a disease that gradually wore him down. But his strong Christian faith and the strong support of his family and friends sustained him to the very end. At the celebration of life held in his memory, his brother, an ordained minister, gave a prayer of affirmation, two of his grandsons read scripture, and his two sons and one of his best friends told the story of his life. It was really a eulogy in many parts. My part was to talk about his church relationship and his faith.

Remembering Maury Sweetin
July 7, 2017

I knew Maury Sweetin for almost 33 years. Not as long as his brother Gary, or his wife Angela, or his sons knew him, but long enough to know him. He was chairman of the Pastor Search Committee that called me to Village back in 1984. We spent thousands of hours together here in church, and thousands of hours together sharing birthdays, or vacations, or holidays, or on the golf course. Last February we played golf together in Florida, just the two of us. Maury knew his days were coming to an end, and he knew that I knew. So, we talked with a candor that was rare for us, even though we knew each other very well. In that conversation, I got a glimpse of Maury's heart. He had a good heart—not a perfect heart, not without the imperfections that all of us have, but a good heart.

Maury did a lot of good through this church. He was a charter member. He and Angela helped build this church—not just the buildings, but the ethos of this church. Maury was a man of ideas, and everywhere I look I see Maury's ideas in place. The memorial garden outside this sanctuary—Maury's idea.

The big green storage container in the side woods—Maury's idea. Julio and company mowing the church lawn—Maury's idea. The electronic church sign out by the road—Maury's idea. The name tag board in the foyer—Maury's idea. The prayer request cards in the pew pockets—Maury's idea. The waiver for the wheelchair lift beside the choir loft—Maury's idea. The connection with Children of Mine and Hannah Hawkins—Maury and Angela's idea.

Maury did more than have a lot of ideas. He served in a lot of roles in the church: charter member, chairman of the Pastor Search Committee—twice, deacon, Sunday School teacher, choir member, offering counter, Personnel Committee member, chair of the Property and Space Commission, preacher! Yes, one time I asked Maury to preach for me on a Sunday that I would be gone.

Maury did stuff that didn't fit into any organizational chart. He was an advocate for immigrants. He helped people find jobs. He wrote a history for the printed program for the 45th anniversary of the church. He helped host out-of-town visitors to our church, such as CBF field personnel Mary van Rheenen and Keith Holmes, and last summer, Oti Bunaciu from Romania, the founder of the Ruth School. Most of all, Maury and Angela welcomed newcomers to our church. From the church house to the original church building to our present building, if they spotted newcomers, Maury and Angela made a beeline to them. And more than once, they hosted baby showers or dinners or other events for young families in our church. Maury was a friend to many.

Maury was a friend to me and Linda. Linda loved him like an older brother. I loved him like, well, I don't know what I loved him like. Maury was not exactly a warm and fuzzy person, although he could get sentimental at times. Let's just say that we respected each other—that our love for each other was expressed in deep respect. He was trying to follow Christ, and I was trying to follow Christ, and as best we could, we followed Christ together.

Maury had so many friends in this church. His best friend, perhaps, was Ron Knode, who died five years ago. They played tennis together and sang in the choir together, and Maury was even trying to get Ron hooked on golf. When Ron died it was a terrible shock to all of us. If Ron were still with us, he would be singing today. We are so grateful that Jeanine sang today because she knew both of them.

Some years ago, after Maury started playing golf, I introduced him to many of my Baptist minister golf buddies. Maury met Jim Langley, Joel Hawthorne, Jerry Buckner, Bob Parsley, Lynn Bergfalk, Gary Javens, and he made connections with all of them. For example, Maury bought a pickup truck from Jerry Buckner. Maury helped Lynn Bergfalk write a grant proposal for City Gate. Bob Parsley went to the hospital with me to see Maury just

Benediction

a couple of weeks ago. And Gary Javens, well, he and Maury made a connection through music. They knew all the popular songs from the Big Band era. We had to be careful about putting them together on the golf course, because a song was bound to break out. They'd be riding in the golf cart together to the next tee box and we'd hear a duet of some old song the rest of us hardly knew. Sadly, Gary died suddenly and unexpectedly about three weeks ago. Now, Maury and Gary (and Ron) are together in heaven. And I can't help but believe that there is some singing going on even now.

Dear Father of the Risen Christ,

With you, there is no death. Our beloved Maury Sweetin has gone from us but is at home with you. And so, our Father, we don't worry about Maury. We know he is in your joyous presence. The journey of his life on earth has ended, and he has now entered into eternal life with you. And so, our Father, we didn't lose Maury. We know where he is. But we are the ones who feel lost. Help us O God, to move through this time of sadness. Help us, not to forget him, but to learn to live without him. Help us to cherish his memory, but to find the faith and strength to carry on.

We pray especially for Angela, for Steve and Anne Marie, for Jeff and Donna, for his grandchildren and his great-grandchildren. We pray for his brothers and their families, for those he knew at work, on the tennis court, on the golf course, here at church. May his example of faithful living inspire us to be faithful ourselves. And may the joy he shared bring a smile to our faces and a lift to our spirits every time we remember him.

This we pray in Jesus' name, Amen.

Reflections

The eulogy for Jim Langley (Chapter 10) was one of the longest I've ever given, and the eulogy for Maury Sweetin was one of the shortest. But it was not short because there was less to say about Maury. It's just that my eulogy was actually Part 4 of a multi-eulogist tribute that included his two sons and one of his best friends.

Maury's son, Steve, told the story of Maury's professional life. The other son, Jeff, told the story of Maury's family life. The friend, Tom, told the story of Maury's relationships with his friends. And I told the story of Maury's church relationships and his faith. Together, the four parts presented a eulogy that provided different perspectives on Maury's life. My part in the eulogy was like the benediction because I sought to affirm our Christian hope and to send us forth with God's blessing.

Maury and his wife Angela were two of our closest friends. We visited them in California after they had moved there for a job transfer. We visited them in Florida when Maury was transferred there for a job assignment, and then multiple times where they spent winters after Maury retired. We were with them in Colorado to visit their son Jeff and his wife. We shared many dinners together in restaurants and in their homes in Bowie and Annapolis, Maryland. Maury and I frequently played golf together. Angela and Linda were "flip-flop sisters," taking yearly vacations to the beach with some other women from our church. Our relationships with them began in the church but went far beyond.

Maury's sons wrote this summary of his life that appeared on the back of the memorial service printed program:

Maury "Mo" Sweetin, 82, passed away Thursday, June 29th at Hospice of the Chesapeake in Pasadena, MD. Maury was born June 28th, 1935 to Tom and Leota Sweeten in the village of Ina, Illinois. The oldest of three children, Maury graduated from Mt. Vernon High School in 1953. Maury served in the Navy as an Electronics Technician. He met his beautiful bride Angela Carpenter near the end of his enlistment and shortly after they wed, he began his career in the aerospace industry. Maury worked aboard satellite tracking ships, then at space flight centers at Cape Canaveral, FL, Gilmore Creek, Alaska, Goddard Space Flight Center, and the Jet Propulsion Lab. Maury became a Vice President at OAO Corporation and only recently retired from consulting work in the aerospace and defense contracting arena. He earned an MBA at Claremont College. He served as a deacon at Village Baptist Church in Bowie and was actively involved in golf, tennis and loved spending time with his grandkids. Our beloved husband, father, grandfather, and great-grandfather meant so much to us that we hardly know where to begin or end when we talk about him and how greatly he will be missed. Dad taught us to serve God, keep our promises, work hard, love our families and care for others. He gave us the dispositions that uniquely combined a great sense of humor with a healthy skepticism of the institutions and bureaucracies around us.

We watched him laugh his way through life's ironies and it became our goal to see the humor in our daily lives. Dad was an idea man. He would see some process or problem that seemed needlessly complex or that begged for a solution and he would solve it in his mind. When such a problem manifested itself around the house, the solution almost always involved duct tape. Dad was a competitor. For the better part of 25 years, he would rise early, quietly leave the house and meet his rivals known to us as "The Earlybirds" at the tennis courts to engage in their version of battle.

Most importantly, we watched Dad love our mother without limits and we learned perhaps our most valuable lesson as husbands from his incredible example. We are thankful to the Lord that Dad got to see all his grandchildren graduate from college and begin careers and start families of their own. That made him extremely proud. We are sad for the loss of such a rare man but we are grateful that we had so many opportunities to live with him, laugh with him, learn from him and love him.

We thank you all for joining us in celebration of his life.

Maury's death was not unexpected. He knew it was coming, and we knew it was coming. Yet, thank God, he remained true to himself to the last. I had a meaningful conversation with him during the church picnic less than a month before he died. I visited him in the hospital about two weeks before he died, and then at home. His time under hospice care was brief. So, his death was a benediction, a good word to the very end.

Chapter 13
At the Cemetery

Burial customs have changed over the years. According to an article in the *Washington Post* (Mar. 5, 2021, A20), in 1960 cremation was rare: Only 4% of those who died in America that year were cremated. The typical burial then involved transporting the embalmed body in a casket in a hearse to the cemetery, followed by a procession of cars. Pallbearers, led by the funeral director, would remove the casket from the hearse and carry it to the gravesite. There the casket would be mounted on belts on a device over the open grave, to be held in place until it was time for the casket to be lowered into the ground. That is still the normal procedure for about half of all burials today. The other half involves cremation.

The cremated remains may be taken to the cemetery in a hearse, or in a private vehicle, or they may not be taken to a cemetery at all. Some people choose to keep the cremated remains in an urn at home, perhaps to be interred or scattered sometime later. Some cremains are interred in a columbarium with individual niches for ashes. Some communities have developed "scattering gardens" for ashes. Sometimes ashes are scattered at sea, three miles offshore, according to Environmental Protection Agency guidelines for a scattering ceremony.

During the early days of the COVID-19 pandemic, I officiated four in-person funerals at cemeteries. Two of those funerals were conducted solely at cemeteries. The third began in a funeral home, followed by a procession to a cemetery for the committal service. The fourth was a committal service in the cemetery chapel. All four funerals involved caskets and in-ground burials. Two of the funerals included pallbearers carrying the casket to the grave, the third had the funeral director and cemetery personnel rolling the casket on a conveyance to the grave, and the fourth had the casket already in the chapel, with cemetery personnel conveying the casket to the hearse after the service.

Two of the cemeteries sought to facilitate social distancing by reducing the number of chairs under the graveside canopy and spacing them out. The third cemetery had the usual setup of about a dozen folding chairs right next to each other in two rows. There was no social distancing for those who chose to sit in the chairs. Most of the attendees, however, stood outside the canopy and tried not to group too closely together. The cemetery chapel limited attendance so that people did not have to sit close together. All the attendees, funeral home personnel, and cemetery personnel wore face masks. I wore a face mask, but in each of the four services, I took off my face mask when it was time to speak so I could be heard. Since I was standing at the head of the casket, and some 15 feet or more or more from the closest attendee, I felt it was safe to remove my face mask for the spoken part of the committal service.

Since two of the funerals were conducted entirely at the gravesite, the transition from the funeral to the committal service was seamless. For the service that began at the funeral home and concluded at the cemetery, there was an extended transition from the funeral to the committal. A part of that transition was the procession from the funeral home to the cemetery, about a 25-minute drive.

Pre-pandemic, I often would ride in the hearse with the funeral director to the cemetery. During the pandemic, I followed the hearse in my own car. Once at the cemetery, I led the procession on foot as the casket was carried to the grave. A violinist played a hymn as the casket was mounted over the grave and people gathered. The committal service began with a brief introduction of our purpose for gathering, followed by a prayer. Then I read a poem and some verses of scripture. Then I offered some words of committal over the casket, followed by another prayer and a hymn played by the violinist. I closed with words of benediction.

I stood to the side as mourners came forward to say farewell, or pray a silent prayer, as they placed flowers on the casket. Then they watched as cemetery personnel lowered the casket into the ground. A few family members came over to me to express appreciation for the service. It was awkward, because there was no touching, no handshakes, no embraces. Then we all got in our cars and returned home.

The committal service at the cemetery chapel had a 15-minute time limit. The chapel was in a veterans cemetery, and the schedule of burials required military precision. The committal was done in the chapel rather than at the grave, again to adhere to the tight schedule. Cemetery personnel would later transport the casket to the grave for burial.

For the three virtual memorial services I conducted during the pandemic, the bodies were cremated and there were no in-person services at cemeteries. The daughter of one of the persons I eulogized lives across the country in another state, and she told me that she intended to return to the East Coast

At the Cemetery

with her mother's ashes when it was safe to travel. In another case, the ashes were interred by cemetery personnel in the family burial plot—but without a committal service. In the third case, the widow and two daughters of the deceased had their own brief time of remembrance at the cemetery where the ashes of their husband/father were buried. There was no clergy or formal committal service, although I had delivered the eulogy online during the virtual memorial service.

Having some type of ceremony at the cemetery helps to bring closure. Whether the body is cremated or in a casket, leaving the remains at the grave allows the family to return home with a sense that they have done what needed to be done.

Thomas Lynch, a funeral director in Michigan said, "A good funeral not only gets the dead where they need to go, but the living where they need to be." When there is no committal service at the cemetery, the process seems incomplete. During the early pandemic, many people died alone in hospitals and nursing homes. Due to safety restrictions intended to curb the spread of the COVID virus, family members and friends could not be with them. One widow told me that seeing her husband take his last breath on FaceTime made his passing even more devastating. Having his memorial service on Zoom allowed people to "attend" who could not travel, but it was nonetheless difficult to feel consoled through a computer screen.

Resuming in-person funerals and memorial services and cemetery committals is an important step toward facilitating the grief process. My guess is that a virtual component will continue to be included in many instances, even though people can now come together. That way persons who are not able to attend the funeral can still participate.

Experiencing community is important in the aftermath of loss. Not only do mourning rituals allow the grieving to say goodbye to their loved one, but they also engender support among family and friends. The loss of a loved one is a lonely time, and the support of others can assuage some of our sense of loneliness. Plus, such rituals can remind us of the presence of God and his continuing care for us. And such rituals can lift up our Christian hope of eternal life.

Cemeteries can be places of comfort and peace. They can be places where we remember that God is with us, and that those who have died have left behind their physical bodies for the promise of a new home in heaven. Thus, gathering at the grave to say goodbye can be the beginning of healing broken hearts. Cemeteries can remind us that the grave is not the end. The resurrection of Jesus Christ from the dead is our hope that life is greater than death.

Committal Service for Ann Rakes
Saturday, September 5, 2020
Fort Lincoln Cemetery, Brentwood, MD

Family and Friends,

We have gathered here in this quiet place of beauty and remembrance to lay to rest our beloved Ann Rakes. We have gathered to remember Ann, but also to place our trust in God, as we say goodbye to this cherished wife and mother and grandmother and great-grandmother and friend whom we loved. Even though there is sadness in this hour, we are not without hope. The apostle Paul reminds us in his second letter to the Corinthians:

> So we do not lose heart. Even though our outer nature is wasting away, our inner nature is being renewed day by day. For this slight momentary affliction is preparing us for an eternal weight of glory beyond all measure, because we look not at what can be seen but at what cannot be seen; for what can be seen is temporary, but what cannot be seen is eternal. (4:16-18)

Ann Rakes was a friend of mine. She and her husband Roy joined our church not long after they moved to Bowie in 1989. Ann had retired from teaching, and Roy had retired from the insurance business, but they both stayed very active. They had leadership positions with the Masons and Eastern Star, and they were faithful drivers for FISH. After they joined our church, they were a tremendous blessing to me and to our congregation—faithful in worship, active in service, devoted in prayer. Ann was a children's Sunday School teacher, and she served on the Education Commission and the Nursery Committee and the Outreach Commission, and she sang in the choir. One of my fondest memories was when their family and friends came together to help Roy celebrate his 90th birthday.

Ann and Roy were married for almost 64 years. They were so proud of their sons and daughters-in-law, and grandchildren, and great-grandchildren. One of the most difficult experiences of their lives was losing their son Jim. But over the years they made many trips to Texas for graduations and weddings to support their grandchildren there. They got to see their Maryland grandchildren more often, and they especially delighted in their great-grandchildren.

After Roy died in 2012, Ann remained in their home in Bowie, and she remained active at church. After about four years, Ann decided to move down to Texas so she could be closer to David and his family. I remember meeting with Ann and David at her home as they were preparing for her

At the Cemetery

move. We sat together in the living room and reminisced and said goodbye. Now we are saying goodbye again. But for us who believe in Christ, it is not goodbye. It is 'til we meet again.

And so, we gather here today because it is time to lay to rest our beloved Ann Rakes. We commit to the earth only that which is of the earth. The Scriptures teach us that our bodies are made of the dust of the ground and to the dust of the ground we will return. But we are more than dust, for when God breathed into our nostrils the breath of life, we became living beings. Genesis 2:7 says, "...the LORD God formed the man from the dust of the ground and breathed into his nostrils the breath of life, and the man became a living being." God breathed his spirit into our temporary bodies, and that is what lives on today. Our physical bodies serve us only as the temporary dwelling place for our eternal spirits. Second Corinthians 5:1,4-5 says,

> Now we know that if the earthly tent we live in is destroyed, we have a building from God, an eternal house in heaven, not built by human hands. For while we are in this tent, we groan and are burdened, because we do not wish to be unclothed but to be clothed with our heavenly dwelling, so that what is mortal may be swallowed up by life. Now it is God who has made us for this very purpose and has given us the Spirit as a deposit, guaranteeing what is to come.

Ann Rakes has laid aside her temporary home. It was made of this earth and to the earth it shall return. But her spirit lives on to eternal life. And now her spirit is in the hands of the same loving God who tenderly cared for her in this life. The Bible promises that one day death will be no more. How we long for that day to come! Until then, may we live in anticipation of the time when we, too, shall lay aside the cares of this life, and take up the joys of eternal life.

> Almighty God, we gather here today to lay to rest our friend and loved one, Ann Rakes. We do so, remembering another grave in another place—the tomb that received the body of our Lord Jesus. As Jesus came from the grave to live again, we know that all who die in him shall never truly die. Thank you, Father, that Ann has finished the course, and that she now has rest from her labors. As we commit her body to the earth, we do so in perfect trust, remembering Jesus' victory over death and knowing, that because he lives, so too, shall we. Comfort our hearts through his words today; strengthen us now with his presence; and may your grace and peace be ours both now and forever. In Jesus' name, Amen.

In sure and certain hope of the resurrection to eternal life through our Lord Jesus Christ, we commend to Almighty God: Ann Rakes. We commit her remains to the ground: earth to earth, ashes to ashes, dust to dust. The Lord bless her and keep her. The Lord make his face to shine upon her and be gracious unto her and give her peace. Amen.

> Servant of God, well done.
> Rest from thy loved employ;
> The battle fought, the victory won,
> Enter thy master's joy.
> ....
> The pains of death are past,
> Labor and sorrow cease;
> And life's long warfare closed at last,
> Thy soul is found in peace.
> *(James Montgomery)*

> Feel no guilt in laughter, she'd know how much you care.
> Feel no sorrow in a smile that she is not here to share.
>
> You cannot grieve forever; she would not want you to.
> She'd hope that you could live your life the way you always do.
>
> So, talk about the good times and the way you showed you cared,
> The days you spent together, all the happiness you shared.
>
> Let memories surround you, a word someone may say
> Will suddenly recapture a time, an hour or a day,
>
> That brings her back as clearly as though she were still here,
> And fills you with the feeling that she is always near.
>
> For if you keep those moments, you will never be apart
> And she will live forever locked safely within your heart.
> *(Anonymous)*

> When you walk through the storm
> Hold your head up high,
> And don't be afraid of the dark.
>
> At the end of the storm
> Is a golden sky
> And the sweet silver song of a lark.

> Walk on through the wind,
> Walk on through the rain,
> Though your dreams be tossed and blown.
>
> Walk on, walk on, with hope in your heart.
> And you'll never walk alone;
> You'll never walk alone.
> *(Oscar Hammerstein II, from the 1945 musical* Carousel.*)*

I have fought the good fight, I have kept the faith, I have finished the race. From now on there is reserved for me the crown of righteousness which the Lord, the righteous judge will give to me on that day, and not only to me, but also to all who have longed for his appearing. (2 Tim. 4:7-8)

There's a hymn that begins:

> There's a land that is fairer than day,
> And by faith we can see it afar;
> For the Father waits over the way
> To prepare us a dwelling place there.
>
> In the sweet by and by,
> We shall meet on that beautiful shore;
> In the sweet by and by,
> We shall meet on that beautiful shore.
> *(Sanford F. Bennett)*

Rest in peace, rest in peace, in God's mercy, rest in peace.

Reflections

The committal service for Ann Rakes took place in Maryland, following her funeral in Texas, where she was living when she died. Then her casket was flown to Maryland where family members from both Texas and Maryland gathered at the cemetery for the burial. Since I had officiated the burials for Ann's husband and their son at that same cemetery years before, the family asked me to conduct her committal.

I offered a brief eulogy for Ann during the committal service. Had the committal immediately followed the funeral, with the same officiant, a eulogy at the cemetery would not have been necessary. But since the burial took place some time after the funeral, and since some participants at the committal did not attend the funeral, I gave a brief eulogy before the words of committal.

Often, I include several poems near the end of a committal service. The poems are intended to convey comfort, but also to allow time for the family and friends to process what has happened. Some find it difficult to leave the cemetery because leaving connotes a sense of finality. The poems provide a few more moments of reflection before the committal service is over and it is time to go.

Sometimes the family will remain at the gravesite after the committal service to watch the casket being lowered into the ground. Not every family feels the need to observe the burial, and not every cemetery can conduct the burial immediately following the committal service. But where it is desired and feasible, witnessing the burial may provide some closure to those who are saying goodbye to their loved one.

Chapter 14
Continuing Ministry

Her name was Kathleen, but most people called her Kat. Her family called her Granny. She was a member of our church, but at first, I did not know her. I was relatively new as her pastor, and we had never met. When the funeral director called me and said that one of our church members needed my services, the name Garvin was not familiar. I checked with our church secretary, and she remembered Kat Garvin. Kat had attended and joined the church years before, but over time she had stopped coming. I found out later that Kat worked most weekends as a real estate agent.

My first meeting with the Garvin family was to plan the funeral for their son, Harry Garvin Jr. The year was 1989, and he had died in his mid-40s after a cancer diagnosis. We had the funeral for Harry Jr., and the following year Kat retired from the real estate business. She started attending worship again on Sunday mornings, and sometimes her husband Harry Sr. would come too. I got to know them, and I really liked them.

Kat was the more outgoing of the two, and she became more and more immersed in church activities. Gradually, I began to meet other members of Kat's family, including her daughters Wanda and Debbie. In fact, Debbie lived next door to her parents, with her husband and two daughters. As her daughters got a little older, Debbie began bringing them to church. Wanda and her husband and their two children would attend on occasion. I also met Kat's other daughter, Jane, and her son, Ronnie, and their families, who lived in other states. Harry Jr.'s death was a great loss, but it reconnected Kat with her church home.

In 1994 the family was devastated by another tragedy when Wanda's husband, Mike Miller, an FBI agent, was killed in the line of duty. The next morning, I went to Debbie's house, where Wanda and her kids had spent the night, to help Wanda tell her son and daughter that their father had died. I got there about 8:00 a.m., but Wanda already had told them. We sat together for a long time, trying to process what had happened.

We began planning Mike's funeral. So many people were expected to attend that the FBI wanted to move the funeral to a larger venue. But Wanda wanted to have the funeral at our church. The FBI set up a closed-circuit camera system so that the overflow crowd at the Catholic church next door could see the service. (This was before virtual funerals on the Internet.) The head of the FBI was there for the funeral, along with the U.S. Attorney General. I met with them in my office before the service. After the service, we processed to the cemetery for the burial. I have never seen so many police cars in a funeral procession. (I tell the story of Mike Miller in Chapter 1 of *Spelunking Scripture: Christmas*).

In 1997, Harry Garvin Sr. had cardiac bypass surgery. I visited him at his home after he was discharged from the hospital and learned that the doctors had discovered he had lung cancer. Harry and I had a heart-to-heart conversation when Kat left the room for a few minutes to prepare some refreshments. Harry died only a few weeks after our visit. We had his funeral at the church. So, in the span of eight years, Kat had lost a son, a son-in-law, and her husband. I officiated at the services and gave the eulogy for each of them. But Kat's faith was not deterred by those losses, or by some significant health challenges. If anything, Kat's faith was deepened.

After a few years of living alone, Kat sold her home and moved in with her daughter Wanda and her children. Eventually Wanda started coming to church with Kat and getting more involved. Debbie had moved away shortly after her father died, but we began to see her from time to time too. Kat would live with Wanda until the end of her life in 2015. I visited with them on several occasions in their home before Kat died. And Wanda would continue her mother's legacy at the church, even to this day.

The ministry of consolation does not end at the funeral home or the church sanctuary or the cemetery. The funeral or memorial service and committal are important rites of passage for the process of mourning, but the ongoing ministry of consolation occurs in relationship. It was my blessing to be in relationship with Kat Garvin for more than 25 years. Her eulogy, which follows here, was an overflow of that relationship.

Eulogy for Kathleen (Kat) Garvin
January 22, 2015

Wanda Miller, in collaboration with her sisters and brother, has written a summary of her mother's life that she has given me permission to share.

> Kathleen Evelyn Sterling was born in Colony, VA, August 4, 1923. The Colony was an institution for epileptics and mentally challenged individuals. Kat's father, James Henry Sterling, had been hired on at the colony to run the

laundry equipment he had installed there, as there was no one else who knew how to do it. Her father died before she was born and her mother, Lottie Garrison Sterling, took over the job running the laundry six days a week, even though she walked with a crutch from having contracted polio as a young girl. Kat grew up in the company of the colony's patients and staff, and because her mother worked long hours, she was raised primarily by one of the residents, Lizzie Caufield. She loved Lizzie as much as her mother.

Kat was the youngest of 6, only 3 of whom survived. Her oldest sister, Mary, was 11 years older and was affectionately known as "Bob," and the middle sister, Frances, known as "Boo," was 6 years older.

Kat attended Madison Heights High School, graduating in 1941. She was voted the most outstanding athlete in her senior class. Although her school sport was basketball, she enjoyed tennis, skating and softball as well, and in later life, coached a softball team.

Mom had many childhood friends that she stayed in contact with until her death. Until 2013, she continued to organize a yearly reunion of the remaining high school class members in Lynchburg, VA. Interestingly, she was the only one of the class members who lived outside of the Lynchburg area. At their last luncheon, six class members were able to attend out of an original class size of 47.

Mom met Dad in high school, and they married the year they graduated. Because of the war, Dad could not get permanent employment. He had been drafted and was waiting for his military assignment and couldn't get hired. He worked at odd jobs like hauling wood. When Dad was finally sent to Germany, Mom went back to the Colony to live with her mother and she stayed there, caring for her mother until 1952 when she died. In the meantime, Jane and Ronnie were born and also lived with Granny Sterling. When Dad returned from his stint in the service, he went to mechanics school at E.C. Glass and learned how to work on automatic transmissions. He got a job in Washington in 1952, as there weren't many mechanics who knew this area of the trade.

They lived in Vienna, VA, where Mom was a stay-at-home mother and where three more children were born. The kids are: Pamela Jane 12/5/41, Ronald Eugene 12/28/42, Wanda Gay 6/5/53, Harry Otha 8/14/54, and Debra Lee 1/30/60. Jane and Ronnie were both married before 1964 when we moved to a bigger house in Fairfax, VA. We stayed there until only a short time because Dad got a job in Maryland. While living in Lanham, Mom began working as a seamstress for a local dry cleaner. She said she needed to get away from the next-door neighbor who constantly neglected her own children to spend all day at our house. She also studied for and got her real estate license in 1966 and began working for Prince Georges Properties.

In 1967, we moved to Virginia Beach because of Dad's employment, and returned to Maryland in 1969 for the same reason. Mom became serious about her career as a real estate agent. She was conscientious, concerned about getting the best deals for her clients and advanced rapidly in her field, being encouraged to go back to school to get her broker's license. When she did, she was hired on as the only female broker for Prince Georges Properties. Some of the other companies she worked for as broker were Baldus Realty and Weichert Realty. She stopped working as a realtor/broker in 1990. Many of her clients were repeat customers, calling her after many years to list their homes or buy new ones, or to have her work with their adult children in purchasing a home.

Around 1971, Mom began attending Village Baptist Church at the suggestion of some of her agents, Effie Gilmore and Ottie Harlowe. She stayed. She felt a real sense of family at Village and particularly enjoyed her "adopted children" there. Her buddies were her favorites.

In 1978, Mom and Dad moved to Woodmore Road in Mitchellville. Dad retired on disability a few years later. They were pleased when Debbie moved in next door and had two children. Their grandchildren could walk to Mom and Dad's across the bridge separating their properties. At this point, four children were married. Pamela "Jane" married John "Jack" Metcalfe. Ronnie married Joan Smith. Wanda married Mike Miller, and Debbie married Don Knuth.

The grandchildren from those marriages are: Eric Garvin 1969, Sheryl Metcalfe 1970, Allan Garvin 1971, Shelly Metcalfe 1972, Benjamin "Micky" Miller 1984, Dale Miller 1986, Emily Knuth 1991, and Erin Knuth 1993.

In 1985, Mom was diagnosed with breast cancer. After she had surgery, she had no recurrence.

In 1988, Harry Jr. was diagnosed with cancer. He had been living with Mom and Dad and continued to stay there, where Mom cared for him until he died in 1989.

In 1994, Mike was killed in the line of duty.

In 1995, Mom was diagnosed with colon cancer. After surgery, she had no recurrence.

In 1997, Dad was operated on for a cardiac bypass at which point they discovered lung cancer. Mom cared for Dad during his recuperation, but he lived only six weeks after the operation.

Prior to his death, he and Mom had decided to move to Calvert County with Wanda and her kids. The house was completed in January 1999. Mom sold her home and moved to Dunkirk in 2001.

Mom also has 10 great-grandchildren who are: Logan Smith 1994, Rehgan Smith 1999, Auston Kranick 2000, Sarah Garvin 2002, Travis Kranick 2002, Sydney Kranick 2003, Abby Garvin 2004, Miles Garvin 2004, Haylee Kranick 2005, Forest Garvin 2005.

Continuing Ministry

In 2003, Mom traveled to Ireland with six family members. In 2011, she traveled to England with two family members. She has visited Canada, Arizona, Oklahoma, Oregon, Vermont, Pennsylvania, New Hampshire, Rhode Island, Georgia, Florida, South Carolina, Iowa, Michigan, Illinois, Minnesota, Virginia, and Tennessee. She has also cruised in the Caribbean. She has spent many summers with family on Delaware and North Carolina beaches.

In 2009, Mom was diagnosed with lung cancer. She had a lobectomy that year and 18 months later, the cancer showed up again in the other lung. Her treatment has been only that which has had little or no side effects.

Thank you, Wanda, for that beautiful tribute. Last Monday, as I met with members of Kat's family, I asked them to tell me some things about her that they would want you to know. Beyond the details of her life that have already been shared, there is much more to say about Granny, or Kat, as most of us knew her.

You might be surprised to know that Kat was a very good athlete. In her younger days, Kat was an excellent tennis player, and softball player, and yes, an excellent basketball player. Even as a grandmother, she would play basketball with her grandchildren, Micky and Dale. Kat was a good roller skater; and she learned to ice skate later in life. Kat learned to water ski in her 40s, and to snow ski at age 50. Even into her 80s, Kat remained physically vigorous. She would climb up on the tractor and mow the grass, or pull weeds, or clean around the house. So, there was Kat, the athlete.

Kat was also a most hospitable person. She opened her home to a variety of guests over the years, some of whom actually lived with the family for a while.

Kat took in her nephew Billy when he was just three years old, and basically raised him until he was 10. Billy later returned at age 17 to live with the family for a time.

Kat opened their home to Sheila and George, a young married couple who lived with the Garvin family for a period of time. Sheila's mother had gone to school with Kat.

Kat welcomed Harry Jr.'s friend, Curtis, into their home. Not just Harry, but all of Kat's children knew that their friends were always welcome in the Garvin home. For a time, a former neighbor from Kettering, Jim Hutchinson, lived with the Garvins.

This "open door policy" was simply who Kat was: she had a big and a kind and a generous heart. When Kat moved in with Wanda and her children, even their friends called her "Granny." So, Kat Garvin was a welcoming person.

As you know, Kat had a very positive, optimistic, spunky personality. It was hard to be around her and not smile. She liked to joke and tease with her family and friends. She used to get into good-natured debates with Wanda's friend Bill about the merits of the Baptist church over the Methodist church. Never mind that Baptists and Methodists are basically "kissing cousins," both having come out of the Church of England and the evangelical tradition. But Kat would get on to Bill for being a Methodist. She also commiserated with him about the Washington football team. Kat could remember the glory days when they were actually fun to watch and root for.

Kat Garvin was an extremely resilient person. She had more than her share of troubles in life—losing her father before she ever knew him, being raised in difficult circumstances, battling several serious illnesses, losing a son, and then a son-in-law, and then her husband. But Kat kept going, and she never felt sorry for herself. In fact, she kept telling me over and over how blessed she was. Kat was one of those people who did not become bitter from the hardships of life; instead, she became better.

Kat was always very strong-willed and determined and independent. The toughest thing for Kat about the last months of her life is that she couldn't do everything for herself, like she was used to doing. But despite her frustrations over her limitations, she was grateful for the help she received from her family and friends.

Kat was a very family-oriented person. She cherished her family members, each and every one of them. She encouraged them, she urged them to further their education, she took pride in their accomplishments, she welcomed new members who joined the family through marriage or birth. Kat loved her children and their spouses, she loved her grandchildren, and she loved her great-grandchildren. She could remember everyone's birthday, and she never stopped enjoying sending each one a birthday card, with a check inside. While Kat was always interested in her family, she never interfered or came across as judgmental. In fact, she was kind of a peacekeeper when it came to the extended family. People respected her—I know I did.

Kat was a woman of deep Christian faith. She joined this church way back in 1971, and she was very active in the early years when John Woodall was pastor. When I first came to Village, I didn't know her, because she was working most Sundays in her real estate job. But after her son Harry Jr. died, I got to know her very well, and she became active in the church once again. In fact, Kat became one of our most active members.

She was in worship every Sunday, except when she was traveling with family to Rehoboth or Ocean Isle Beach or Vermont or overseas—like that fabulous trip she took to Ireland to celebrate her 80th birthday. Kat really enjoyed Dave Thompson's Sunday School class, and she attended special studies that I led, such as our annual Lenten Bible Study and a study on Baptist history and beliefs.

What I appreciated most about Kat was her heart for others. I can't tell you how many newcomers to our church that Kat reached out to. She was always so friendly, so welcoming, so encouraging. She had a heart for young people, especially children and teenagers. We have a "Buddy Program" here at the church that links adults with children and youth. Kat didn't have just one "buddy"—she had a host of them.

As I said, Kat was a person of deep faith, and her faith in Jesus sustained her throughout her life. The good care that she had received from her daughters and other family also sustained her to the very end.

After I learned that Kat had died, I started contacting people who I knew would want to know. I called Jo Reiter, and Jeanette Robinson, who had known her longer than I had. I called the Parrecos, who are vacationing in Florida, and I sent an email to Maury and Angela Sweetin, who are wintering in Florida. Maury emailed me back on his cell phone. He simply wrote: "Sad news, but she had a great life and cheered many of us along the way"— Maury Sweetin.

Maury said in 16 words what I have been trying to say in many more. We are sad that Kat is no longer with us, but she did have a great life, and she did cheer many of us along the way. Of course, her passing is painful for all of us who loved her. But there was no sign of Kat suffering. She went to sleep Saturday night with her daughter Debbie close by, and she woke up Sunday morning in the arms of God. Now, she has left behind her worn-out earthly body, and received a new and perfect spiritual body. Her faith has been fulfilled, and she has heard her Savior and Lord say: "Well done, good and faithful servant, enter your Master's joy!"

Of course, there is sorrow in the hearts of those she has left behind. Kat was a faithful wife, a loving mother and grandmother and great-grandmother, a devoted sister, a caring mother-in-law and aunt and great-aunt, a good friend, and her going leaves a hole in our hearts. But we are comforted by many precious memories and by the promise that she has received her heavenly reward. Kathleen is truly home, at rest and at peace with her Father in heaven.

Now, may God grant those whom she loved, and those who loved her, the grace to carry on, in the sure and certain hope of the resurrection from the dead, to all who have placed their faith in him.

Tribute to Mother
By Frances Johansan (adapted)

She painted no Madonnas
on chapel walls in Rome.
But with a touch diviner
she lived one in her home.

She wrote no lofty poems
that critics counted art.
But with a nobler vision
She lived them in her heart.

She built no great cathedrals
that centuries applaud.
But with a grace exquisite
her life cathedraled God.

Reflections

Some eulogies are the overflow of an ongoing relationship. Such was this eulogy for Kat Garvin. Ironically, the first funeral I officiated for the Garvin family, for Harry Jr., was before I knew them. By the fourth funeral, for Kat herself, I knew most of the members of the Garvin family. Even those who lived in other states I got to know over time as they would come back for subsequent funerals or for family visits. One Sunday Kat's son Ronnie and daughter Jane came from out of state, and after worship we took a picture of the whole family with Kat.

After my book, *Preaching for the Long Haul: A Case Study on Long-Term Pastoral Ministry,* was published early in 2020, Kat's daughter Wanda asked me to inscribe copies for her siblings. I received a note from Wanda's sister, Jane, who lives in Pennsylvania. In the note Jane wrote:

> Thank you so much for your book. I have thoroughly enjoyed your sermons. You have meant so much to our family, having given special services for my Mom, Dad, brother Harry Jr., and brother-in-law Mike. You know my Mom cared so much for you and Linda and Village Baptist.

Yes, and Linda and I and Village Baptist cared so much for Kat. Giving the eulogy for someone you love is an honor and a privilege and a holy calling. It was my honor and privilege and holy calling to give eulogies for many people

Continuing Ministry

I loved during my 33 years as pastor of Village Baptist Church. Since I retired in 2018, I have continued to give eulogies for people I loved.

> In Chapter 10 of *Preaching for the Long Haul*, I begin with this confession:
>
> By far the hardest part of being a long-term pastor is saying goodbye to people you love. I'm talking about more than announcing my retirement. I'm talking about saying goodbye over the course of thirty-three years to people I loved. Of course, every pastor must deal with losses. But because relationships deepen over time, the loss seems greater when those deepened relationships end.

I am a barefoot eulogist because I seek to speak a good word while standing on holy ground.

About the Author

Bruce Salmon served for 33 years as pastor of Village Baptist Church in Bowie, Maryland, a suburb of Washington, D.C. During that time, he preached almost 1500 original Sunday morning sermons, and officiated at many funerals and memorial services for parishioners, their family members, his own family members, and members of the community.

A native of Fort Worth, Texas, Salmon received a B.A. with a major in English from Baylor University; an M.Div. and a D.Min. from The Southern Baptist Theological Seminary; and an M.A. in Counseling Psychology from Bowie State University, with a specialization in Clinical Pastoral Counseling.

Salmon served on several committees of the D.C. Baptist Convention and several commissions of the Baptist World Alliance. He has written multiple volumes in the Bible study series, *Spelunking Scripture*, and is the author of *Storytelling in Preaching* and *Preaching for the Long Haul: A Case Study on Long-term Pastoral Ministry* (Nurturing Faith, 2019).

After retiring from the full-time pastorate in 2018, Salmon has continued to conduct funeral and memorial services for members of his former church, friends, neighbors, and people needing a pastoral presence in the aftermath of loss. He considers bereavement services one of his most important ongoing ministries.

Salmon is husband to wife Linda, father to grown children Amy and Marc, father-in-law to Stacey, and grandfather to granddaughter Ford. In addition to studying the Bible, his interests include spectator sports, music, museums, golf, and travel.

Other Books by Bruce Salmon

Spelunking Scripture: Easter. Nurturing Faith, 2022.
Spelunking Scripture: Acts and the General Epistles of the New Testament. Nurturing Faith, 2021.
Spelunking Scripture: Christmas. Nurturing Faith, 2021.
Spelunking Scripture: The Letters of Paul. Nurturing Faith, 2021.
Storytelling in Preaching: A Guide to the Theory and Practice. Broadman Press, 1988.
*blog on www.spelunkingscripture.com

www.ingramcontent.com/pod-product-compliance
Lightning Source LLC
Chambersburg PA
CBHW071006160426
43193CB00012B/1940